Angelic HEALING

Change your life with help from the angels

JENNY SMEDLEY

CICO BOOKS

LONDON NEW YORK

Published in 2014 by CICO Books
An imprint of Ryland Peters & Small Ltd
20–21 Jockey's Fields   519 Broadway, 5th Floor
London WC1R 4BW   New York, NY 10012

www.rylandpeters.com

10 9 8 7 6 5 4 3 2 1

Text copyright © Jenny Smedley 2014
Design and illustration copyright © CICO Books 2014

A CIP catalog record for this book is available from the Library of Congress and the
British Library.

ISBN: 978-1-78249-113-2

Printed in China

Editor: Anya Hayes
Designer: Alison Fenton
Illustrator: Trina Dalziel

For digital editions, visit www.cicobooks.com/apps.php

Angelic
HEALING

An angel will love you even when you can't love yourself

CHRISTINE CLARKE

Contents

Introduction

What Are Angels?

Many people would love to be able to heal their lives with the help of angels, but sometimes they have no idea what angels really are, or how they can be called upon for help. Angels are described as "messengers" that exist to enable communication between us and God, but it's not obvious how they might be contacted. In order to communicate on their level we need to "raise our vibration," but what does this really mean in a practical sense? I will try to explain.

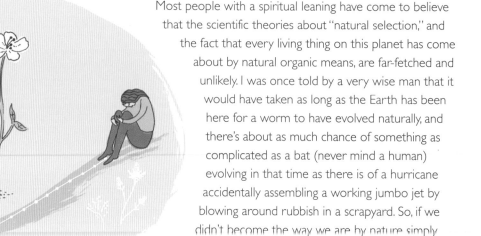

Most people with a spiritual leaning have come to believe that the scientific theories about "natural selection," and the fact that every living thing on this planet has come about by natural organic means, are far-fetched and unlikely. I was once told by a very wise man that it would have taken as long as the Earth has been here for a worm to have evolved naturally, and there's about as much chance of something as complicated as a bat (never mind a human) evolving in that time as there is of a hurricane accidentally assembling a working jumbo jet by blowing around rubbish in a scrapyard. So, if we didn't become the way we are by nature simply selecting the best "blue-print," then there must be some other explanation. There must have been some off-worldly intervention.

An alternative universe of angels

Many scientists also now accept that we live in a multidimensional universe. It's obvious that other beings must inhabit these alternatives, and must interact with us, maybe even interfere with us, whether guiding our evolution or guiding our everyday decisions and lives, or what would be the point of them being there?

Over 68% of the known universe consists of something called "dark matter," which is a completely unknown entity—no one is able to explain what it is, or how it works, or what it's for. The mystical cosmos is a great deal more strange and mysterious than we ever thought possible. We simply do not have all the answers. Perhaps dark matter could be where angels exist and work?

In fact, the explanations for all these things involve angels.

People will describe angels variously as benevolent or supernatural beings. But no one really explains why these beings would want to help humans, or why humans have the right to expect them to. Why would some divine being care if you get the job you'd like, or meet your soul mate? Surely they would have better, more important things to do? In fact, angels are much more than unreachable beings separated from us by a spiritual divide. What happens to us has a huge bearing on them too.

The angel–human connection

People often think that angels are the souls of loved ones that have passed over and come back to visit, but in fact angels have never taken human form. Angels operate on an entirely different stream of consciousness from that of humans, and naturally occupy other dimensions to us. It's my belief that some levels of angels are actually connected to us on a very deep, although sometimes elusive, level. I believe that these angels help us because they want to evolve and change themselves. Imagine existing as a divine being, whether you were an all-powerful god or an angel. Imagine that you have existed forever, and will continue to exist forever. Try to sense what that would feel like. Humans are much baser beings than angels. Just think how boring it really would be to live forever, with nothing ever changing, with you never growing or learning. Most of us get bored doing nothing for more than 10 minutes, so imagine what that would be like for angels who exist forever, unchanging. Angels need to progress, like every other entity in the universe. Stagnation is surely worse than death. In their divine pure energy form, in whichever dimension they exist in, there is nothing that angels can learn from as they are already complete in their development—there is no way for them to evolve or change. So they (or God, if you like) created us, and that is why they help us. It was once decided by some higher power that angels needed to experience a different way of being—to be able to experience emotions, triumphs, disasters, even vicariously. They needed to learn things that an immortal being cannot understand, let alone learn. In order to do these things they needed a place to experience them, a place where physical beings equipped with heightened emotional capacity lived. So it came to be that they created us and this planet.

Soul Angels

I have had information downloaded to me by angels that we, in our physical human bodies, are here to host sparks of what I call soul angels. These angels want to experience life as a part of a human in order to learn and grow, and we carry that tiny spark of them within us. Therefore their evolution depends on ours. If we evolve and succeed, then so do they, and this is why they help us. Our evolution depends on us making the right choices, and experiencing things in the right way. Angels will help us to do this, because they need to. Our evolution is their evolution.

Angelic stowaways

So, we all have angels we can call on, and they want us to call on them. However, it isn't always a simple process. For one thing, we need to be spiritually evolved enough to ask for their help—we have to be able to make this choice, retaining free will and the ability to make mistakes, hence the need for us to reincarnate. As we know, these angels operate on a different level of consciousness to us, and have to be reached by us deliberately connecting and communicating with them. By journeying with us, they do not inhabit our being, nor are we able to inhabit theirs, so we can't automatically access their consciousness. They are more like an invisible, often unsensed, passenger, something like a benevolent stowaway. This stowaway is not in constant mental contact with us, but is hovering above, viewing what we experience from a distance.

Contacting our stowaways

How do we get in touch with these angelic stowaways? We need to contact them in order to ask them for their help to change our lives and heal our pain, whether it is physical, mental, or emotional distress. We need to engage with the dimension that angels inhabit, lifting our own consciousness at least part way to theirs in order to meet them halfway. How is this possible? All dimensions have a pulse, a rhythm. The Earth itself has a pulse, caused by a convection process that comes from within it, and we who live here naturally synchronize with it, or we couldn't survive.

Understanding our planet's energy

Our planet has a slower pulse than the dimension that angels live in, and normally our pulse or energy matches that of the planet we live on. Not being synchronized with this pulse permanently could be what caused mass extinctions in the history of our planet. If you have any doubt about this pulse, notice how animals are more finely attuned to the natural pulse of the planet than we are, and how much stronger their intuition and instincts are than ours. Animals are renowned for anticipating natural disasters, such as earthquakes and tsunamis— the news often reports on how the animals all fled just before the catastrophe struck. This isn't because they could hear something we couldn't, it's because they could sense something we couldn't: the pulse of the planet changing because of the approaching event. People have mostly lost the ability to do this.

However, with the right thought processes, and the right activity of brain waves, we can still actually speed up or slow down our pulse, temporarily lifting it out of the Earth realm. With very few exceptions we're not capable of achieving the same high-level vibration as angels, but we can get close enough that they can meet us halfway, and communication can begin.

Angels Throughout History

All modern and ancient religions talk of angels, and a lot of New Age religions are based entirely upon them. Beings that are recognizably angels have been part of the human belief system for more than 6000 years, predating the Hebrew faith.

Angels of all kinds have been recognized by different cultures through the ages, and here are some examples:

* The Ancient Greek god Hermes had wings on his heels and was called the "messenger" to the gods. The word "angelo," from which "angel" derives, is Greek for "messenger," thereby linking all modern angels back to Hermes. Before this time, angels were known by other names.

* Beings known as the Karibu were worshipped in Babylon 4000 years before the birth of Jesus.

* In the belief system of the Incas, angels were referred to as Earth Guardians, as the Incas' way of living was strongly connected to protection of the Earth's energies.

* Mayan sculptors carved statues known as "Mayan Angels." These beings had wings, a familiar physical characteristic of how we recognize angel form.

* Native American Totem poles often have a figure known as a "Thunderbird" at the top, an indomitable angel-like spirit, who brings messages from other worlds. This mighty being is an omen of war—its beating wings bring the sound of thunder in the heavens, representing warring spirits in the skies.

* The Inuits believe that all things have a soul—everything is infused with energy and spirit, which persists after death. Anirnisiaq is the word understood to mean "angel" in Inuit mythology.

How Can We Contact Our Angels?

How do we raise our pulse, tune in to the angels' frequency of vibration/energy?

1   Meditation—the controlling of your thought patterns to bring about lower brain waves (lower brain waves equaling higher vibration)—is a tried-and-tested method. Some find solitary meditation difficult, having trouble switching off their mind and internal dialogue from everyday matters. One way to circumvent this is to join a meditation group, because as with any form of praying, the energy of a gathering is often more powerful than that of one person alone.

2   Laugh as often as you can.

3   Sing—especially something inspiring and positive.

4   Dance—by moving in a synchronized, joyous way, you free and stimulate your body's energy.

5   Stand and look at a thing of beauty, whether it be a piece of art or a spectacular sunset, and allow the emotion, appreciation, and unconditional love you feel for it to flood your body.

6   Take deep and cleansing breaths. Do this over and over, in a restful place with no distractions, until you feel calm and serene.

7   Talk to your angels—out loud. Be honest and say how you're feeling.

8   Look for signs that relate to how you're feeling and what your needs are—these signs can be subtle, such as a certain song coming on the radio, a feather appearing at your feet in an unusual place, or someone you were thinking of calling you on the phone or bumping into you in the street

9   Angels can be light anomalies, orbs in photos, strange shapes in clouds, or rainbows. The more you accept and learn to recognize these signs, the more you will notice them.

10   Light a candle and use the flame as a focus. The flame acts as a signal to your angels, and tells them that you want to communicate. In time you can find your own personal signal that will get your angels' attention.

11   Make a point of saying some kind words to someone. It really can positively change their day and in turn lift your energy.

12   Energy travels, and you can easily pick up negativity from others. There may be certain people you dread bumping into, or getting a call from. I call these people "psychic vampires," as deliberately or accidentally, they suck out your good feelings and slow down your vibration. So, stay away from negative people as much as you can.

These methods are a slow build rather than a sudden epiphany. They work gradually, and you'll experience the added bonus of your own life and emotional state improving too, as you begin to notice messages from the angels guiding you as to which decisions to make.

Seven Signs to Know When Your Angel is Near

1   When you're happy most of the time. Angels love the sound and energy of a joyous heart, and will always be drawn closer to it.

2   You feel a brush on your shoulder, or goose-bumps on the back of your head.

3   You have a sensation that feels like cobwebs across your face.

4   You see the same numbers over and over again, on clocks, in phone numbers, on cars—absolutely anywhere.

5   A whisper in your ear or your mind stops you from doing something rash.

6   A delicate note fills your ears when there's no music playing.

7   A strange "coincidence" opens a door you thought was closed.

Shut down any negative thoughts or feelings. This will take a lot of effort and concentration at first, until it becomes purely automatic to do so. When you can do this, you can also be sure that your angels are listening. Of course it should always be remembered that while one might be able to connect with one's soul angel, and successfully ask them for help, there will be times when for our best evolution, what we're asking for is not actually what we need and it may appear that our questions have not been answered. However, if you find that's the case, you should also remember that angels rarely close a door without leaving a "window" open. In other words, if you don't appear to get exactly what you've asked for, look carefully around to see if an alternative has been provided. Don't be closed-minded, or you could miss a great opportunity.

Dear Soul

You are a ship at sea and I am the light in the lighthouse. When all seems dark and stormy, and you feel lost and alone, cast your eyes beyond the rocks and see me as a spark of hope on the horizon. As a human you sometimes lose track of your rightful path and you stumble as you make your way along your life's journey. Let me be the one to lead you because my light will never dim. Let me be the one to lead you home to a happy and fulfilling life. Lean on me and I will never let you fall.

Your Angel

Angels are not there beside you for just a minute or an hour or a day,
but forever and always, the most faithful friend you'll ever have.

CHAPTER I

The Healing Angels

I'M A FIRM BELIEVER THAT YOU DON'T NEED TO KNOW THE NAME OF A SPECIFIC ANGEL IN ORDER TO RECEIVE HELP FROM IT. IF YOU ASK IN THE RIGHT WAY, YOU WILL GET THE RIGHT HELP. I ALSO BELIEVE THAT AS ENERGY BEINGS THEY DON'T USE SPECIFIC NAMES FOR ONE ANOTHER. HOWEVER, WE HUMANS OFTEN NEED TO HAVE A FOCUS FOR OUR ENERGIES, AND NAMES CAN BECOME THAT AID. BELOW IS A LIST OF THE NAMES OF THE VARIOUS ANGELS, AND WHAT THEY ARE TRADITIONALLY SAID TO HELP WITH. AS YOU WILL SEE, ALL THE ANGELS CAN HELP IN SOME FORM OF HEALING, WHETHER IT BE PHYSICAL, SPIRITUAL, MENTAL, OR EMOTIONAL. THESE ARE THE ANGELS MOST COMMONLY CALLED UPON TO HELP US IN DIFFICULT TIMES OF EMOTIONAL TURBULENCE.

Anael: This angel will help you if you tend to obsess with your own "small stuff," and let your life flash past without concentrating on it. Anael encourages you to slow down and appreciate beauty around you. Once your life has slowed to a reasonable pace, you'll find you have increasing amounts of time to look around, and stop missing life's small miracles. This may have a beneficial effect on your health—many illnesses and diseases can be caused or worsened by a racing, stressed mind and body. This heightened mindfulness and appreciation of life may also make us more attractive to the right kind of partner, one who will nourish and heal us.

Azrael: This angel is known as the angel of death. However, this should not be a fearful thing. If we contemplate dying, most of us would only wish that our passing be easy, painless, and among those we love. This angel can bring healing energies, easing our worries and escorting us on a rush of gentle wings to the afterlife, where we will meet our loved ones who have gone before. To have any confusion and fear eased by an angel's comfort at this time would be a blessing. It would be much better if we could avoid long-drawn-out illness, if that is the right thing for us, so this angel's intervention could often be a mercy.

Castiel: This angel is the one to call on if life seems to be stuck in a rut, and the mundane quality of it is leading to depression. Castiel can give us the will and the courage needed to see opportunities, take chances, and make changes. It can be difficult to take a leap of faith, especially if depression ensures that any action at all can seem like a monumental effort. People often find change, whether in relationships, jobs, lifestyle, or any other area of our life, quite a challenge. Moving to a strange place, especially alone, is a very daunting prospect. This angel is able to help ease our fears and generate a sense of adventure.

Chamuel: Known as the angel of peaceful relationships, Chamuel will help you to resolve conflicts with others, and forgive people who have hurt or offended you. Chamuel is particularly helpful in repairing misunderstandings in both personal and work relationships. This angel will also enable you to make the right decision when faced with a difficult choice. As anyone will know who has experienced teetering between two paths, weighing and reweighing the options in front of you, the mental anguish is tremendous. Indecisiveness, or a lack of faith in your own decision-making process, causes mighty internal conflict that can lead to depression and a conviction that you never get things right and always make bad choices. This angel will enable you to be your own leader and to make the right decisions for your path through life.

Gabriel: This is the angel that deals with blockages of all kinds. For instance, Gabriel helped me with writer's block, as you will read later. This is the angel to call on if you are having trouble conceiving, another form of blockage. Your body may need to recover from a past-life trauma if you experience problems getting pregnant. There might have been a difficult experience in a past life giving birth, or you could have suffered the torture of losing a child, in which case your subconscious could be instructing your body not to get pregnant. Gabriel can unblock these past-life traumas and heal your soul, so that you can fulfill your dreams in this lifetime.

Jophiel: Call upon this angel if you have very low self-esteem. We are all truly beautiful within. Even if we consider ourselves physically unattractive, or unintelligent, or if we have been brought up to be unkind on the surface, we must remember that all souls at their most fundamental level are unconditionally beautiful. Low self-esteem can occur because we behaved badly either earlier in this life, or in a previous one. Jophiel helps us to learn from our previous errors and allows our soul to heal, revealing our true inner beauty.

Marmoniel: This angel is described as being "he who holds the clouds in your hands." To me this means that he can give you the power to influence the world about you. If you feel deep down that you have some higher purpose you're here to achieve, then this angel can help you to take steps toward it. If you feel that doors are going to be shut on you because of your upbringing or lack of education, this angel can walk you to your destiny, despite your misgivings. This angel can also heal those who have physically survived terrible times, but who are still wounded emotionally, and give them the confidence to enjoy life again without fear.

Michael: Traditionally known as the "warrior angel," he is also the angel of justice. If you feel embittered through being wronged, and in danger of being negatively driven by revenge, then Michael can assure you that those you seek revenge against do not need to be punished by you. He can give you courage to face challenging events you'd rather not have to go through, such as surgery, examinations, tests, or public speaking. Michael will protect and heal your sensitive nature, allowing you to have the courage to face these intimidating circumstances, and to fulfill your destiny without losing the sweetness of your personality.

Oriphiel: This is the angel that can help you to function mentally and intellectually. If you're reaching an age where your memory is failing you, or stress is making it impossible for you to concentrate on your job, this angel can help you to cope. By healing your mental processes and allowing you to focus on the right areas, this angel can bring you back to a life you can enjoy. This angel will also protect you if you're seeking connection with someone you're grieving for, by guiding you through any pitfalls and leading you to true communication with spirits.

Raguel: This angel's specialty is healing of the planet. Humans have done great damage over generations, and although some of this is beyond our salvation, we can do our bit to limit the extent of the damage in future. If you dream of being an eco-warrior, this angel will help you in your quest. This angel gives us strength of character and resolve. This is the time for us all to stand up and be counted when it comes to protecting the Earth and all that live here, so if you have this noble goal, connect to Raguel and use the might of the angels that created this world to heal it.

Raphael: If cruelty and lack of compassion toward others is something that makes you feel ill, then Raphael will help you to cope. If you'd like to get into charity work, or some other altruistic cause, this angel will help you to gain the means you need to do it. When some people long for power it isn't always to help themselves—they long to be powerful in order to help others. This angel helps those people, and will heal them should their aims change and they begin to view the wealth and fame resulting from their good deeds as the final aim, instead of the means to an end.

Saphiel: This is the angel to call on if you have a bad temper, and always seem to be in conflict with those around you. Having a red rage is a form of illness, and one that makes it difficult to interact within a civilized society. It often comes from having lived an ancient "dog eat dog" kind of life, when it truly was survival of the fittest. The soul that constantly feels great anger has somehow bypassed the memories and learning of past lives, and needs to be reminded of gentler lives, when having compassion and trust was the best way to live. By healing the temper, this angel can bring serenity to the life of this person and those around them.

Uriel: This is the angel to call on to help you communicate with angels! You may have trouble believing, or perhaps switching off your conscious mind in order for communication to start. Try asking this angel for help at the start of any attempt to connect. With a calm mind, use this name as a trigger to raise your vibration. This angel will also heal any tendencies to blame others for our own shortcomings. Perhaps you have a noisy neighbor, and you blame them for your not being able to communicate with the angels. This angel will help you to be able to connect and lift your consciousness away from worldly distractions, no matter what is going on around you.

Angels have many forms. As energy beings they can appear in any guise they, or we, wish them to. For example, one young girl I channeled an angel for had hers appear as a unicorn. I think this was because it was the form she could connect to best. We should bear in mind that angels can be called by any name we, or they, choose. If you want to make up or channel a name special to you, and just between you and your angel, that will be just as successful as choosing one of the names above. The key things to remember are not to over-analyze anything, and always that angels know best. If you persist with calling only one particular angel, you might actually be missing out on the best one for you. So leave the details to them.

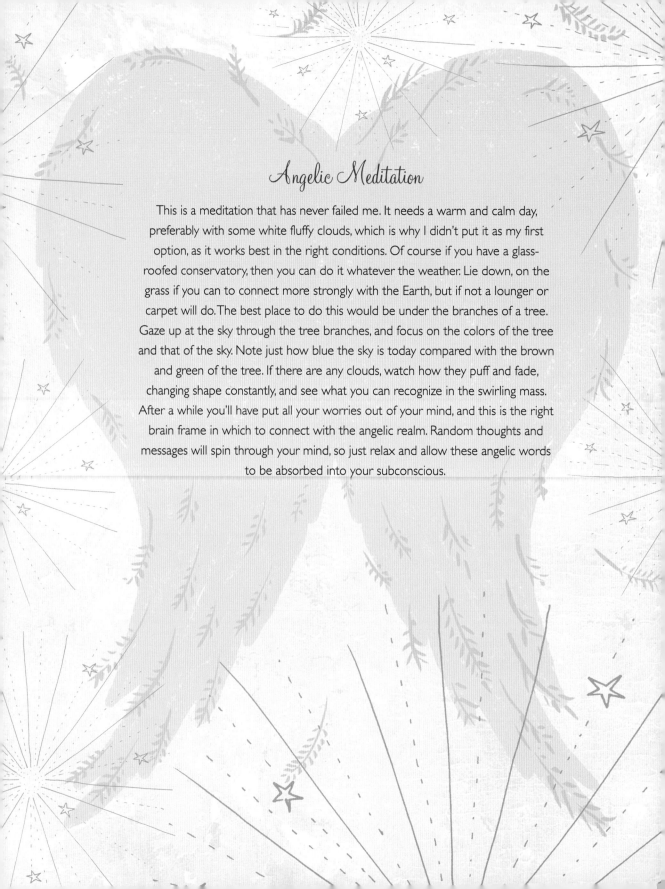

Angelic Meditation

This is a meditation that has never failed me. It needs a warm and calm day, preferably with some white fluffy clouds, which is why I didn't put it as my first option, as it works best in the right conditions. Of course if you have a glass-roofed conservatory, then you can do it whatever the weather. Lie down, on the grass if you can to connect more strongly with the Earth, but if not a lounger or carpet will do. The best place to do this would be under the branches of a tree. Gaze up at the sky through the tree branches, and focus on the colors of the tree and that of the sky. Note just how blue the sky is today compared with the brown and green of the tree. If there are any clouds, watch how they puff and fade, changing shape constantly, and see what you can recognize in the swirling mass. After a while you'll have put all your worries out of your mind, and this is the right brain frame in which to connect with the angelic realm. Random thoughts and messages will spin through your mind, so just relax and allow these angelic words to be absorbed into your subconscious.

CHAPTER 2

*True Stories of
Angelic Healing*

ANGELS REALLY ARE ALL AROUND US, HELPING US, GUIDING US, AND KEEPING US SAFE FROM HARM. YOU NEED ONLY LOOK AT ANY NEWSPAPER TO FIND ACCOUNTS OF ANGELIC INTERVENTION THROUGHOUT THE WORLD. HERE ARE JUST A FEW STORIES THAT I HAVE HAD SENT TO ME.

Talking with the angels

An edition of *Newsweek* featured a story about a neurosurgeon, Dr Eben Alexander, who went into a coma for seven days after contracting bacterial meningitis. Dr Alexander told reporters that, contrary to expectations, he had remained conscious during the "coma," but in another place. He says that during this time he was conversing with beings in heaven, including angels, who sang and spoke to him.

A miraculous escape

It was reported that a retired magistrate from the north-west of England once had her life saved by an angel. At the time she was in her 30s, driving home from a party—a 45-minute journey, with her husband and two other passengers. She hadn't been drinking because she knew she'd be driving home, but still she fell asleep at the wheel. It was about 5am when the car left the road, hit a fence, and turned over, coming to rest upside-down. The driver's side of the car took the full impact of the crash, and should have killed the driver, as it was totally crushed. However, strangely she was catapulted out of the car as it turned over, in the opposite direction to the roll, and landed some 20 feet (six meters) clear. Stranger still, her neck was broken, but she wasn't paralyzed. Crash investigators couldn't understand how she had escaped. Her husband and the other two passengers walked away totally unhurt. She credits angels with removing her safely from the car.

Rescued by an angel

A cave-diver was in the Bahamas on a research project when she suddenly realized that her safety line had detached. She said her heart rate went so high it was actually making her vision "bounce." To make things worse, she was already in a bad emotional state as her husband had only recently been killed, in a diving accident in the Red Sea. She despaired, expecting to die alone and afraid. She sat down on the floor of the underwater cave she'd been exploring, and waited for certain death to come. But then the cave lit up with words of light that drifted through the water, and she recognized the words as something her husband had often said to her— you have to believe you can, because if you believe you can't, then you can't. She calmed down immediately, feeling that he was there for her, and then saw a silver thread, which she was able to follow to safety. She felt her husband had been brought to her by an angel.

Angelic guides

A man who suffered from claustrophobia took his two young sons on a skiing trip. The mountain scenery gave him a great sense of free, open space, and they were all enjoying the holiday. With little warning, an avalanche cascaded down on top of them, and they were all plunged into darkness, being separated and tossed around, until they didn't know which way was up. It was hard for them to breathe as they were totally enveloped in the snow. Expecting to be numbed and made helpless by his claustrophobia, and almost giving up, the father was sent a terrifying vision. He was shown his sons being unloaded from a plane at their home airport, in coffins. This vision snapped him out of his helplessness and, somehow knowing which direction his sons were, he found the power to plough his way through the snow and rescue them. He firmly believes that an angel sent him the vision, in order to give him the strength and determination he needed.

Saved by a guardian angel

A boy was out on his bike one day when he lost control on a canal path. Before he could avoid it, the bike bounced over a low wall and catapulted toward the dirty water. As he sailed through the air he could see the water below him, and saw that he was going to land on some kind of metal spike, which looked like part of some railings. He curled into a ball to try and save himself from being damaged by the bike and railing, and heard the splash as his bike hit the water. He shut his eyes in anticipation of his landing, and the next sensation was a thud, and a roll that winded him. When he opened his eyes, he wasn't in the water as he'd expected to be. Instead, he was back on the bank, on the grass, meters from the wall. He said it was as though something caught him in mid-air and threw him backward. He believes it must have been his guardian angel.

An angelic hero

An elderly woman was shopping in New York and taking an escalator downward at Macy's, when she suddenly tripped. As she fell, she knew she would break her hip and it would be the end of her independence. In that moment she was consumed by grief, but suddenly, a man showed up at the foot of the escalator, caught her in his arms, set her up on her feet, made sure she was okay, and then disappeared right before her eyes. She looked all around to thank him, but he was gone. She is convinced that he was not human, but an angel.

My recent experiences with angels

I've had numerous angel experiences over the years, and will continue to do so, as long as I ask for their guidance. As a writer, I occasionally feel blocked, unable to release my creative juices. This can be very troubling. Imagine if you were a lawyer, and suddenly felt unable to recall the details of the law one day! On one occasion when troubled, I asked my angels to help me, and then closed my eyes. I was transported in my mind to an underground lake. I was in a boat, paddling across a flooded cavern. I could see the stalactites reaching down toward the water, the surface of which glittered, as if lit from below. On the far side of the water I could see an angel waiting for me. He told me his name was Gabriel, and that he would be my inspiration if I ever got blocked again, and would prevent it from taking hold. I have honestly never been blocked again.

The hare and the deer

Angels will often use animals as a medium to communicate with us. My husband and I were recently thinking of moving across the country to be closer to family, which was a tough decision. We loved our home dearly, and loved the rolling countryside of Somerset, in the south-west of England—both of which would have to be left behind. So, we traveled east to our proposed destination, Norfolk, in order to see how we'd feel living there. One morning I took our dog, KC, for a walk across some fields, and was delighted to see both a hare and a deer. The hare was loping across a stubble field, and the deer appeared briefly on the track right beside us, before darting away again. The hare is recognized to symbolize creation—in our case, a new life in another area of the country. The deer was a Muntjac, not a native animal, but one that has inhabited a new place and thrives there. Another appearance happened when I was viewing a potential home. I was looking out of a bedroom window into the garden, when a second Muntjac deer stepped into view, just a few meters from me. All the family saw it. I took this to mean that we would be happy in that property. Then, when I was journeying back to Somerset on the train, a red deer, which is a native animal and very much at home in Norfolk, stood gazing at the train, at my window, as the carriages rolled past. I took these signs to mean that we would have a great new life in Norfolk, we would be successful at uprooting ourselves, would find the place welcoming, and would settle there happily. And so it has proved to be.

The helpful bluebird

All I knew about Sedona in Arizona before I went there was that it's been voted America's most beautiful town, and that it's the New Age Center in the USA. My husband, Tony, and I decided that as we hadn't had a holiday for five years, we wanted to go somewhere spectacular. Sedona got the vote. We were also hoping to have a spiritual experience. As it turned out, we wildly underestimated the power of where we were about to visit.

Sedona is an oasis of green in the middle of the hot, dusty Arizona countryside. It's surrounded by the most beautiful, wind-sculpted, red rocks, all of which have names inspired by their shapes, such as Cathedral, Bell, Castle, and Kachina Woman. There are four powerful energy vortexes in the area, each one near a different red rock.

A vortex is an invisible whirling funnel, created by the motion of energy emerging from the earth. This energy leaves a measurable residual magnetism in the places where it's strongest, and can have a marked effect on anyone even slightly sensitive to such things. The energy interacts with the inner person, bringing the necessary balance of male or female energies to that person. An interesting side effect of the vortexes is that juniper trees respond very strongly to them. The closer the trees are to the energy, the more their branches grow with an axial twist in them, as they follow the spiral of the funnel shape.

As we drove into Oak Creek Village, on the outskirts of Sedona itself, we had no idea where the vortexes were. I suddenly found myself moved to tears by, I thought, the mere beauty of the place, and we discovered only later that we were passing right between two vortexes at the time. That experience was just the start. The place is extraordinarily beautiful. Most houses are built adobe style, their rounded walls rendered in colors that blend perfectly with the surrounding rocks, making them appear to have grown there naturally. There is even an egg-shaped house.

Our first close encounter with a vortex was that of the Cathedral Rock, which can be reached by driving to the Red Rock River Park, and then walking through the trees to the river with its stepping-stone crossing. The soil is red, the water is red, and the rocks are red. Cathedral Rock towers over you. Tony and I sat and meditated, asking for any messages we might need to feel or hear. I was told, quite clearly, "You may communicate, but not here. We are gathering at Kachina Woman."

The Cathedral Rock vortex imparts female energy, whereas the Kachina Woman vortex brings balance, giving you more male or female energy, depending on what you need. You can't see Kachina Woman from the road as it's hidden by a knoll, and it's quite a difficult walk without a guide, as the trail is not at all clear. We set off from where our car was parked, and soon became quite lost. Bear in mind that the temperature was 100 degrees, and that Arizona has rattlesnakes, scorpions, and tarantulas, and you'll understand why we got more than a little nervous.

I felt my heart start to thud in my chest as the reality of the possible danger of our situation hit home. There we were, lost in the desert—we had told nobody where we were going, so nobody would come looking for us. We had no water and were surrounded by heat, rocks, and deadly wildlife. It's incredible really how what seems so safe when you're in the middle of town suddenly turns very scary almost in a single step as you walk out of civilization and into the wild. The parking lot had been empty, and although it was quite a short distance away, there had been no other cars there, so no one would hear us if we shouted for help, and we had no idea which direction it was in.

Luckily, we were obviously being watched over, because just as I was about to really panic, a small bluebird appeared on the ground in front of us. He cocked his head as if to say hello, and then hopped along between two trees. He came back and did this repeatedly, until, trusting that he was angel-sent, we followed him. He hopped along, and cocked his head repeatedly, as if to make sure we were following, and before long we came to the Kachina Woman Rock. We were very relieved, and the bird disappeared, leaving us to wonder if we would ever find our way back to civilization!

We stood and meditated (not feeling it was advisable to sit on the ground with the possible creepy-crawlies about). The messages were wonderful, assuring us that things were going to work out, and as the energy swept through us we felt transported back to an era when the Earth was worshipped and venerated, and the area was peopled with noble races that should never have been driven out.

Sure enough, we had no idea how to find our way back to the car, but once again our little bluebird angel appeared, and led us back to the part of the track that was well-worn enough to follow.

Dear Soul

Never fear to tell me your deepest, darkest secrets, for I already know them, and yet I love you still completely and unconditionally. I can do nothing else, for you are a part of me. I see you as an intrepid warrior, forging your way through the difficulties of being human. It is not easy to be human and yet retain your spiritual self. You and I may lose touch along the way from time to time. But know that I am a constant for you. I am like a river that runs alongside you, and even though at times you may venture off down a different channel, you will always find your way back to me when you're ready, and I will be waiting.

Your Angel

Angels do not judge you, nor do they make demands or impose conditions, for you are all angels at your root and one day you'll return to that part of you in triumph and a burst of golden light.

CHAPTER 3

Angelic Reiki with a Twist

REIKI IS A GOOD EXAMPLE OF HOW A TRADITIONAL HEALING TECHNIQUE CAN BE ENHANCED WITH AN ANGELIC TWIST. I HAD THE OPPORTUNITY TO SPEAK TO AN ANGELIC REIKI PRACTITIONER AND TWO OF HER CLIENTS. I'M REALLY GRATEFUL TO HER CLIENTS— AND TO ALL THE PEOPLE WHO SHARED THEIR EXPERIENCES WITH ME. NOT EVERYONE IS WILLING TO SHARE THEIR STORIES OF ANGELIC HEALING, WHICH IS A SHAME AS I FEEL THIS CAN REALLY HELP OTHERS IN NEED WHO MAY BE A LITTLE WARY, OR EVEN AFRAID, OF TRYING ANGELIC HEALING. IT IS SOMETIMES HARD TO PUT INTO WORDS EXACTLY HOW ECSTATIC YOU FEEL WHEN IN THE PRESENCE OF AN ANGEL.

What is Traditional Reiki?

The word Reiki comes from the Japanese for "universal life energy." The tradition was founded by Dr Mikao Usui in the early twentieth century. He did much research on the subject of healing, and dedicated his life to creating the basis of the Reiki we see today.

Dr Usai's healing methods are built on the fact that we, and everything around us, are comprised on a quantum level as energy. If this energy is able to flow freely, then our bodies should be healthy, but blockages in the system will create areas prone to illness. The person receiving the treatment does not remove any clothing. They can either lie down on a massage table, or sit in a comfortable chair. They don't need to do anything except relax. The Reiki practitioner will adopt certain positions with their hands, which are placed near, but not touching, the client's body. The treatments can be as short as 45 minutes, or may take over an hour. No practitioner should try to give any medical diagnoses. Sometimes patients might feel some heat or tingling, but others may not have any physical responses at all. However, they should feel relaxed and calm at all times.

Angelic Reiki

Glenda Bouchere is a member of the Angelic Reiki Association and the British Complementary Medical Association (BCMA). She'd previously been practicing Usui Reiki (as described above), when a lady at a healing conference told her she thought Glenda would enjoy learning Angelic Reiki. She's now a Master/Teacher of Angelic Reiki, and absolutely loves it. She says that during this therapy she channels angelic healing through her hands, which are placed on the client. The healing energy, which comes from the angelic realms via healing angels, archangels, ascended masters, and galactic healers, flows into the client automatically to the area where it's most needed.

Glenda says her clients often tell her after a session that they have truly "drifted away" during it, and are surprised at how long they've been in the session, as time becomes impossible to judge. Her clients always feel really great after the sessions, and some feel they had a spiritual experience. Physical and mental problems should feel greatly improved during the days afterward.

This healing also affects the therapist. Glenda says it makes her feel completely at peace during the session, and she also feels a loss of time. After the session, she will pass on any messages she senses the angels have given her (excluding medical advice.) She feels loved and content afterward, and never feels drained, as the healing is channeled through her and not from her.

Case Study
Angelic Reiki

KERRY SAID:

I'm 38 years old and have suffered severe depression. I was on medication for
about 20 years. Then two years ago I went to see a lady who did an Angel card reading
for me, and it literally changed my life. The angels told me to ask my doctor if I could try and stop
taking my medication, as it was toxic and harming me. Whilst I was there the angels
sent me healing, and it really helped. I had a Reiki session with the same lady, and since that day I've been
a different person. That was two years ago and I have not taken one tablet since then. My life has changed
and moved forward, and it's all for the positive. I now talk to my angels daily, through meditation, CDs, and
cards, and I surround myself with crystals and other positive things.
I have also undertaken the first degree in Reiki myself.
I'm now a positive person with a great outlook on life. I still have days when I'm not as happy as
"normal," but nothing like before, and I'm sure everyone has days like that! That lady and the angels
really did change my life; I couldn't be happier since I've not been on medication.

Case Study
Angelic Reiki

CARLY SAID:

I'd broken my jaw, and conventional medicine was not helping much, especially with the pain. Angelic Reiki had been recommended to me and I decided to try it, and despite having been quite skeptical I could really feel a difference afterward. Glenda chatted to me beforehand, and explained that I just had to relax and listen to the music, and she'd let me know when the session had finished. I listened to the most beautiful music, and I must have drifted off because next thing I remember was Glenda calling my name. I felt so relaxed, as though everything in my body had been treated. Glenda spoke to me about the session, and made sure that I was fully grounded. Every Angelic Reiki session has helped me to improve, and the effects go on for several days following the treatment.

It made me realize we're not alone, and there's always something else there to help us, much greater than we think. I feel it's the angels, but others might feel something else. A number of friends have experienced Angelic Reiki with Glenda and have told me similar things. I've also seen pets benefit from this treatment. The feeling it gave me doesn't really leave me. It's made me look at my life in a different way. I'm more optimistic and try to see the higher picture.

Case Study
Angelic Reiki

RICHARD SAID:

I've had a permanent long-term back problem since childhood, and it gives me a lot of pain and discomfort. I know that Angelic Reiki won't cure the problem, but it does provide great relief from the pain, and makes me feel much more comfortable. It's a very enjoyable and relaxing experience as well. I started having sessions of Angelic Reiki with Glenda following a recommendation from a friend. It's more comfortable for me to sit on a chair rather than lie down for treatment, but Glenda assured me this wouldn't affect my experience. There was some relaxing music in the background, but I was not aware of much else throughout the session. I was a bit "spaced out" after it finished, but Glenda made sure I was grounded, and we then discussed my experience. I feel more comfortable now, with greatly reduced pain, and emotionally I feel relaxed and happier. Also, I visit a chiropractor and he commented on how well I was doing shortly after one of my Reiki sessions. I'm certain other people could enjoy the same experience as I do.

Angel Healing From the "Food Angel"

This is a totally unique "add on" concept, created by Ceri-Ann Beecroft. I asked her why she called herself the "food angel." It doesn't mean she's a New Age dietitian, just that she believes angels are as essential to our wellbeing as food is, and she tries to supply their energy.

It all started when Ceri-Ann was very ill with ME, and her partner bought her a magazine called *Angels*. She read it, and also a book that came free with it. The subject of angels struck a chord with her, and she started to ask them questions. Her connection with them grew steadily, and now she sees angels, and works with their colors when healing and doing clearings.

She says that working and living with the angels and their guidance has completely changed her life. She began to train in courses that she'd always dreamed of, and continually keeps working to bring her goals to fruition. She has seen the most amazing things happen, and has gone in for many things she would never have been brave enough to do previously. She hosts her own radio show, has written a book, and has visited sacred places.

In her opinion, every person can have a wonderful experience with angels if they're open to it and trust. She says that because we have free will, we have to ask for help from angels; they will not approach us, even if we are in need, unless we communicate with them. It's also up to each individual person to be brave enough to go ahead with the suggestions and opportunities that open up to them once they have expressed their desires and hopes to their angel. They must take the leap of faith and begin to grow as a person, and listen to the intuition lovingly provided by angels.

Ceri-Ann believes she brings a unique flavor to her treatments because of her personal experiences. Her clients usually feel a sense of great peace, and see colors during their sessions. Ceri-Ann can actually see the angels working with her, and their colors pouring into the body she's working on. She expects to see the whole person change in the way they talk and carry themselves afterward—as though they've had a spring clean, and full-body service. Clients should feel clean, lighter, and brighter, and a special type of healing will be activated in their body itself. They can be made more comfortable in more critical conditions, and surrounded by love and safely travel to the other side, if it's their time to pass.

I asked Ceri-Ann to describe her practice, and what clients could expect at her sessions: "When I'm healing, I call in the angels that I intuitively know I need to be working with in the session. Using my third eye, I 'see' the angels and the specific color of the energy pouring through. My hands are laid on the client, or hover just above them. Sometimes I'm called to give areas extra attention. I call through to the angels and speak their healing, thanking each angel in turn. I feel the love and I feel the presence of guides helping during the clearing."

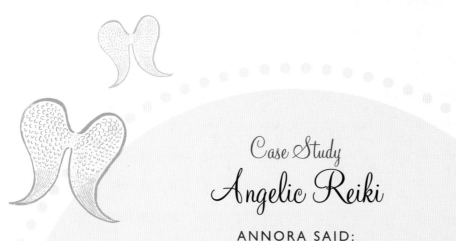

Case Study
Angelic Reiki

ANNORA SAID:

I was seeking answers and enlightenment following the death of my parents.
I already knew that Ceri-Ann was a very spiritual person, and wondered if she'd
be able to help me understand things more clearly.
Because I'm also an angel therapist, albeit without the many years of experience Ceri-Ann has,
I was happy to visit someone else who worked with angels. Ceri-Ann helped me to find my path in life,
as I was very lost, confused, and feeling very alone after my parents died. Many of us have
felt the same way after such a loss, but perhaps have not known where to find help. I hoped that
Ceri-Ann would be able to help me shine a light on certain messages I'd been getting. I needed
confirmation because I was afraid that, in my grief, I might have only been seeing what I wanted to,
and that I might be missing the true interpretation of the signs. Physically, during the session I felt like
a huge weight had been lifted from my shoulders. I felt a tickling sensation on the back of my neck, that
I later came to understand was a visit from my dad. I had a tingling sensation, almost like pins and
needles, in my right hand and both feet, which I know now was the energy most likely of my
mom, or my Spirit Guide, or angel. I felt a warm flood, almost like a hot flush but without
feeling clammy, and I think this was the love embracing me as I became able to unblock my
mind, and accept the messages I was getting.

The session was extremely emotional, as I'd been holding on to so much
negative energy since my mom and dad passed. I felt the negativity dissipate almost
immediately, and as the session progressed, I felt comforted, warm, loved, the complete
opposite to how I'd been feeling when I asked Ceri-Ann for help. I'm quite an emotional
person, and so I was quite surprised that despite the release of emotion I was feeling, I didn't cry.
I was just taken over by euphoria, because I was so happy to have a clear understanding of
events and occurrences.

Today I'm mentally in a much better place. Before this, although I was peripherally aware of the
great love of higher beings surrounding me, I'd felt almost like I wasn't included in it, that I was
an outsider because I hadn't had a good relationship with my parents, and thought that they'd gone to
their higher realm with animosity or bad feeling about me. Now that I know that isn't the case, I'm able to
see things more clearly, able to reminisce without anger, and without feeling lonely. I understand now that
things were as they were, even though my parents longed to change them. I understand that my parents
love me, are very proud of me, and are with me. I'm able to be aware of their visits and the signs they
leave for me, and I'm open to their love, able to welcome them.

If it hadn't been for Ceri-Ann, I'm not sure where I'd be. Ceri-Ann encouraged me on this path
I now follow, and offered guidance, enlightenment, and hope. It feels like she's pulled me back
from the edge, and has helped me to understand so much. I'm far more relaxed and no
longer have as many disturbed nights. Ceri-Ann furnished me with the tools
to dig my way out of a hole I'd been languishing in since 2007,
when my father passed away.

Case Study
Angelic Reiki

MARY SAID:

Ceri-Ann was recommended by my friend for her work, and angels intrigued me so I decided to have a home visit. I'd lost my son and always felt the angels were helping me through tough times. I also have cancer and am open-minded about treatments and therapies, but believe that my personal connection to the angels led me to Ceri-Ann. On the day that my son passed over, I was woken by a feeling of urgency. I reached his room just as he looked at me standing at the door, and then he passed over. My dear boy was gone on his eighth birthday. My other children were my focus, and I had to keep it together for their sakes, and spiritually I had dreams of angels that were helping me heal, and assuring me that I still had much work to do here. I often feel my face being stroked, and temperature changes around me that are inexplicable. My children and my faith have helped me through, and I have had times when things seemed to be moved around on their own and I got messages in my sleep. I also often experience a quick flash of light, that makes me realize I'm not alone in this.

I'd been experiencing pain in my jaw, as a side effect of the tablets I had to take for my bone cancer. I'd had two medical procedures which had failed, and am due another one, which I hope will be third time lucky. Ceri-Ann chatted to me and sat with me while I related my problems, then I was made comfortable, and music was softly played in the background. I was aware that Ceri-Ann was calling in angels and talking to them, and I was then guided into a meditative state. During the treatment I saw colors such as blue and green, gold and red, while Ceri-Ann was speaking and healing. Then I felt tearful, but very happy, as if something was shifting. I felt light and unloaded. I felt everything become free almost immediately, and the pain dwindled. I eventually fell into a sleep that lasted a couple of hours, and felt great from then on.

After a few sessions, I feel more energized and in a good frame of mind, which is very important when you're working with an illness like cancer. I'm building on my angel collection and expanding my knowledge, and I feel very happy and rejuvenated. You can't help feeling better after being in Ceri-Ann's company; you just lift, because she has this incredibly positive presence. She's helped me so much with my mental state. And physically, I don't know how it works, but it just does. I recommend anybody to try it, as they'll be surprised at how they will feel thereafter. It's helped me very much.

Angelic Meditation

Choose a special crystal; or rather let one choose you. When I first started working with angels through crystals I was amazed that when I held or sometimes just passed my open hand over crystals, the right one would cause a pinprick of heat or cold, or a sharp tingle in my palm, telling me that this was the one I needed. The best crystals for this are those that have a lot going on inside them. Rainbows will appear most readily in fluorite and quartz, and once you focus on looking inside them you will start to see worlds within worlds, galaxies within galaxies. I like to ask troubled people, a few seconds after they begin to study their crystal, "what are you thinking right now?" The answer is always "nothing." This is the state of mind you're looking for. We all have the ability to connect with angels when we are children, but life gets in the way and we lose it. By emptying your mind you allow angels in. So, having chosen your stone, just sit or lie comfortably and stare into it. The angels will come.

CHAPTER 4

Angel Therapy with a Twist

"ANGEL THERAPY" IS A COPYRIGHTED MODULE CREATED BY RENOWNED ANGEL EXPERT DOREEN VIRTUE. SHE DESCRIBES IT AS FOLLOWS: "ANGEL THERAPY IS A NON-DENOMINATIONAL SPIRITUAL HEALING METHOD THAT INVOLVES WORKING WITH A PERSON'S GUARDIAN ANGELS AND ARCHANGELS, TO HEAL AND HARMONIZE EVERY ASPECT OF LIFE." SINCE DEVELOPING THIS HEALING MODALITY IN 1996, DOREEN HAS TAUGHT THOUSANDS OF PEOPLE WORLDWIDE HOW TO ENGAGE IN ANGEL THERAPY. MANY OF THESE STUDENTS HAVE BECOME ANGEL THERAPY PRACTITIONERS THEMSELVES.

Angelic Therapy with Crystal Rituals

Nikki Byford has developed her own way of healing through angels. She believes that in a past life in Atlantis she was using this same method, and has been guided by her angels to recall it and put it back into use. Nikki told me that she'd always felt drawn to Atlantis, and as a child in this life she remembered standing at the bus stop with her mum wondering why on earth they had to wait for a bus, and couldn't just "transport" to where they needed to be. When visiting the doctor and hearing about operations it always felt so invasive and unnecessary to her, and she wondered why they had to do this. It seemed bizarre to her, and at the time she had no idea she was connecting to her life times in Atlantis.

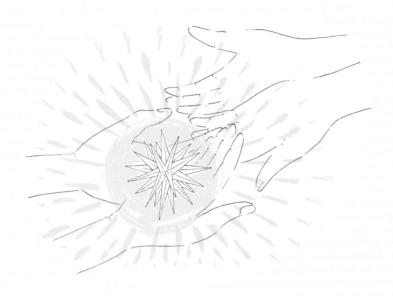

It all started to come together one day when Nikki was carrying out a Reiki treatment on a friend. She began to see the beginning of what she thought was a new treatment. As soon as she started channeling these Crystal Rituals she instinctively knew they were from Atlantis, because they felt familiar somehow. Her clients' reactions confirmed this for her as they too moved intuitively with her, completely understanding what she was doing. Often they see, hear and experience the same things. Every time she completes a ritual she gets the strongest feeling wash over her that she and the client have done the same thing before. She also gets flashback images of working in Atlantis. In them she's in a temple with a huge clear quartz crystal in the ceiling, and as the sun shines through, beautiful, colorful rays of light stream down to the beds the patients are lying on. This powerful image created and still creates today a divine, sacred space in which to work. After the treatment in Atlantis, friends and family would be waiting outside the room, and when the patient had completed their ritual it would be time to party and celebrate to embrace and honor the new blessings and gifts.

During the weeks after her discovery, she channeled more and more information until it was completed. Today she uses 10 different treatments working with 10 angelic realms. Crystal Rituals are a complete journey, which harnesses your own empowerment. Within each treatment, the client lets go of something old, and welcomes in beautiful new guidance from the angels. Within the angel treatment Nikki concentrates on helping her client to let go of others' negative words, comments, or actions made toward them. The angels describe it to Nikki as cleansing away the mud from our hearts and souls. By holding onto others' comments we can't move forward and so can't step into our own divine power. Nikki says the angels want the very best for us so the treatment is like an angelic "shower" using a selenite wand, massage, and hands-on healing. Some of

her clients say they actually feel as if they walk with, talk to, and hold hands with the angels. In the end all the upsets should be washed away and replaced with a deep sense of peace and tranquillity, and clients can see a clear path ahead of them.

Nikki says that when she does the treatment she actually feels the emotions behind the upsets, even though she isn't told anything personal. She also sees colors and divine white light pouring into every cell of both her and her client.

I asked Nikki to sum up what she felt about her work. She said, "When my ladies leave they often say they feel they can achieve anything. I've been so blessed to be given such an amazing treatment to dispense and I know this is my life's work. I feel my clients' essence and I see their light. It feels like we're going on their magical journey together, hand in hand. And I love watching their progress and seeing them step into their own divine power." Each time Nikki does a treatment, she understands it on a deeper soul level and it all makes perfect sense to her. When she first started her journey, she had many questions. How come I can see things? How come I can do healing without any training? How come I know things about people, and why do they come to me and tell me things? The Crystal Ritual was the missing part of the puzzle, and now she completely understands it all, and feels truly blessed and honored to be able to share it.

Case Study
Angelic Therapy

ANNE SAID:

I knew that I needed some type of spiritual support and healing as I had been going through a tough time emotionally, so I asked the owner of a local crystal shop for a recommendation without even explaining why. He suggested that Nikki could help me, and he was right. The first couple of times I went we agreed that I would have nurturing and supportive treatments. I needed to heal and stabilize before I'd be ready to start again on a new journey through my life. Then when I felt ready, I'd start Crystal Rituals, and once I did the journey certainly began! In the first session I experienced such a deep sense of clearing that it's impossible to describe, and I experienced distant past-life memories, both visual and physical. They were so clear and so familiar then, although I'd never been able to access them so well before, and once I felt them, knew what had happened in the past, I was able to let it go, back into the past where it belonged. Afterwards I felt healed and integrated to my core, ready to move forward, ready to open to new things from a position of wholeness and strength. Each treatment has been just as profound, but each has been completely different. Sometimes I'm able to describe what has happened, but usually I don't need to, because Nikki will already know. It's extraordinary, but she seems able to see what I'm experiencing just as clearly as I do. The sense of protection I gained from the angel sessions allowed me to feel fundamentally differently about being in the world, and the strength I gained from the goddess treatment allowed me to complete a task that I had been struggling with for over a year. To have a spiritual "team" behind you is a quite remarkable experience. However, it's the fairy session that has been the most wonderful because of the freedom it has allowed me to be playful again—it's life-changing already, and I'm only halfway through!

Case Study
Angelic Therapy

CHRISTINE SAID:

I've known Nikki for about five years, and wanted to try her therapy because I know she works with angels and also crystals, which I love. I was drawn to crystals after my Reiki attunement some years ago, and I always say they chose me to work with them, not the other way round. I love angels because I feel they're loving and protective, but I was not as familiar with them as I was with crystals.

The treatment itself was extremely relaxing and full of love. Nikki speaks at the beginning to explain what we're doing, and that the purpose is to start getting rid of old memories, habits, and thoughts we've been given over the years, which we don't need. She calls in the angels to help, and the energy in the room is beautiful.

During my treatment, I started off sitting in a chair and Nikki used a selenite wand to massage my head, which was incredibly relaxing and calming. After this, I lay on the massage bed and Nikki massaged my hands with oil. Then she used the selenite wand again. I think by then I'd drifted off into a dreamy state. I personally didn't see angels, but I saw colors, mainly royal blue. I felt quite "floaty" afterward, which was rather nice! I could have spoken during the treatment if I'd wanted to, but I was too relaxed to speak.

I wanted to try the treatment because I sometimes lack confidence, and I was keen to get rid of any restrictions embedded from the past. This treatment does just that, as it washes away old negativity and enables a new beginning. The treatment definitely set me on a more positive course. I'm more open and accepting, and feel more secure that I'm being loved and looked after, which has helped my self-confidence.

I have since tried different therapies with Nikki, all of which are uplifting and healing.

Case Study
Angelic Therapy

LORRAINE SAID:

I met Nikki through a mutual friend and, when I learned that she worked with crystals,
I booked in for a chakra rebalancing session with her. This was such a wonderful, gentle therapy
that I wanted to try some of her others. I'd seen her Crystal Rituals advertised in a crystal shop, and
asked her about them. She explained what each one was about, and they sounded so different from
other therapies that I'd experienced, being a blend of the spiritual and the physical,
that I was very excited at the prospect.

The first one was very relaxing, but it was the second one, meeting and working with angels, that really
made a huge impression on me. I'd often enjoyed guided meditations, either listening to a CD or in a
meditation group, but this was like a guided meditation especially for me. Nikki doesn't speak during the
treatment, so the journey I went on and the messages I received came into my mind without any verbal
suggestion from her. While she gently treated my physical body with beautiful crystals, my mind
enjoyed a wonderfully uplifting experience. Regarding the physical side of the treatment, I'd just add
that it is an incredibly gentle therapy and Nikki is very caring and respectful in all physical
contact with her clients.

I went on to have all ten of her Crystal Rituals, each one unique and inspiring. I had
always believed in angels, but I am aware of a stronger connection now. Nikki's
treatments relax and soothe the body, but, more importantly, they have
definitely enriched my spiritual life.

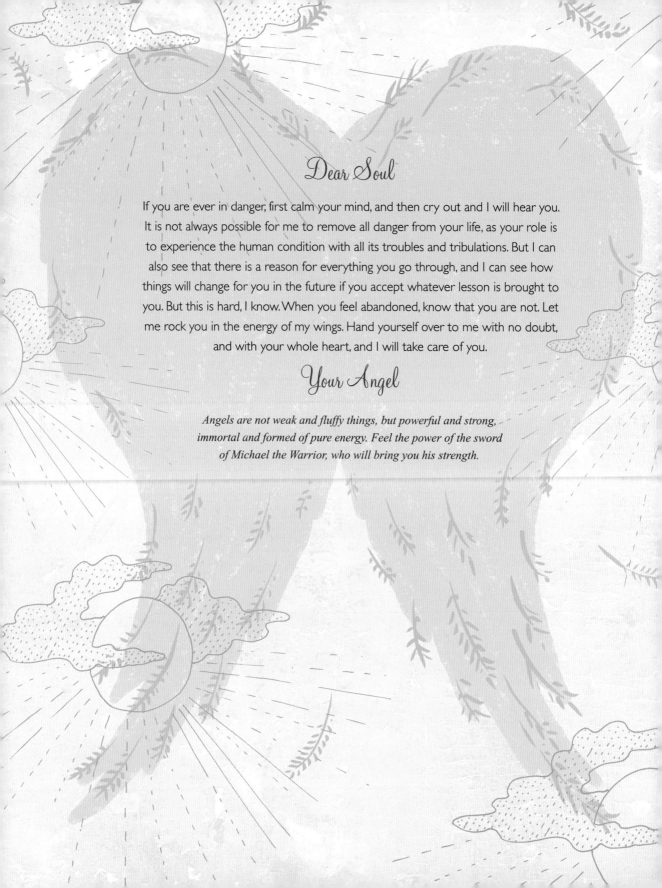

Dear Soul

If you are ever in danger, first calm your mind, and then cry out and I will hear you. It is not always possible for me to remove all danger from your life, as your role is to experience the human condition with all its troubles and tribulations. But I can also see that there is a reason for everything you go through, and I can see how things will change for you in the future if you accept whatever lesson is brought to you. But this is hard, I know. When you feel abandoned, know that you are not. Let me rock you in the energy of my wings. Hand yourself over to me with no doubt, and with your whole heart, and I will take care of you.

Your Angel

Angels are not weak and fluffy things, but powerful and strong, immortal and formed of pure energy. Feel the power of the sword of Michael the Warrior, who will bring you his strength.

CHAPTER 5

Angelic Healing of Your Past—with a Karmic Twist

DURING CONVENTIONAL PAST-LIFE REGRESSION/HEALING, THE THERAPIST PUTS YOU INTO A STATE OF DEEP RELAXATION SO THAT THEY CAN SPEAK TO YOUR SUBCONSCIOUS MIND, WHICH STORES ALL EXPERIENCES YOU'VE EVER HAD. THE FOCUS IS NOT ON YOUR CHILDHOOD IN THIS LIFETIME, ALTHOUGH THAT MAY BE A PART OF IT, BUT RATHER ON WHAT HAPPENED TO YOU A LIFETIME AGO, OR EVEN MANY LIFETIMES AGO.

Angelic Karmic Healing
Kim Hutchinson has always had a strong desire to help people, coupled with an affinity for the spiritual. The angels initially came to her following an impassioned conversation with God, during which she asked for the ability to help heal the world. Several angels appeared and told her that they'd been with her throughout her life. They explained that they'd been conversing telepathically with her since she was a child. Now that she was an adult, the angels helped her to embrace her clairaudience (the ability to hear spirits), and also to develop her other extrasensory gifts, including her capacity to heal. The angels also guided her to earthly teachers, and helped with practical matters, opening doors so that she could set up her healing business.

Kim started her healing path by giving angel readings. Prior to giving these readings, she had studied Reiki and other forms of energy healing. Although these healing modalities did not fully resonate with her, they did help her to enhance her intuitive gifts. Kim discovered that she could act as a channel for the angelic realm, and, over the course of several years, she has "downloaded" a lot of past-life information during her readings. Past lives had always fascinated her, and her interest in them led to the karmic healing.

Understanding Kim's gift
People who were interested in past lives gravitated to her, and inevitably would ask if she offered past-life regressions. Naively at first, she started to practice regressions on her husband and friends, which didn't always achieve the desired result. She also learned that there's a risk of people getting "stuck" in past-life trauma when the treatment is performed by an

inexperienced practitioner. She immediately stopped the regressions, and yet the requests for help with karmic healing poured in. She realized she didn't know how to help people.

Naturally, her angelic friends came to the rescue again. They told her about their karma healing technique, which they simply call past-life healing. They explained that the potential dangers inherent in regressions could be minimized, or even eliminated, by healing the person first, before providing them with past-life details. They also recommended that she act as a witness for patients, to prevent them from re-experiencing their prior trauma. Both of these techniques are vital, as they allow the patient to release their karma in the present instead of getting stuck in the past.

What happens at a healing?

Each of Kim's healings is unique, as the angels customize the treatment to suit the individual. However, the healings do share several commonalities. For a start, they're all distance healings, meaning she performs them remotely. She lets the recipient know how to prepare in advance. She then asks the person to send her the issues they want to release, along with a recent photograph, preferably one showing their eyes, as these are the gateway to the soul. At a mutually agreeable time, Kim begins the healing process by inviting archangels Raphael, Michael, and Raziel, and the other angels of healing, along with the recipient's guardian angels and higher selves, to facilitate the healing. She also checks with the recipient's soul to ensure that the healing is in their highest interest. If so, she sets the intention, to be a crystal-clear channel for the divine, and then she goes into a deep meditative state. On the spirit plane she meets with the angels and the person's soul.

Starting the process

The angels may perform an initial healing at the start of the process, depending on the patient's needs. Typically, they take people to a healing facility in their realm such as the Crystal Palace (an angelic crystalline structure used for sound healing), or to a natural environment such as a waterfall. Water, crystals, music, energy, and love are frequently employed in the healing process. Kim assists with the healing by using her intuition, along with her training in energetic and angelic therapy.

Once the patient's energy is clear, Archangel Raziel enables the karmic healing by helping them visit past timelines, although everything happens in the present. Kim may visualize the client moving through a tunnel, over a bridge, or spinning in a vortex of Archangel Michael's creation. As they enter each of the past lives, the setting will be momentarily obscured by fog. The mist then dissipates, and a scene plays out featuring the client in a previous incarnation. Kim observes every detail as closely as possible so that she can share this information with the patient after the healing. In a typical session, the angels will take Kim and the client to around six past lives, although there may be as few as three or as many as 12. The angels, in their immense wisdom, know exactly which past lives should be recalled, and are adept at balancing any painful memories with joyful recollections. At the end of each painful visit, the angels will heal whatever issues arise. For the positive incarnations, they energetically transmit the happiness to the client. There is vital information to be gleaned from both painful and positive memories. Perhaps there's a past-life connection with a person or place. Maybe the person has a skill that could be used in their present life.

Returning to the present

After the past lives have been explored, the client returns to the present timeline. Their wellbeing is reassessed, and if necessary, they receive another healing. At this point, Kim emerges from her dream state. Before she forgets any details, she immediately makes a recording of all her observations. The information she receives is usually detailed and specific. She then emails a digital file to the client so that they can listen to it after they've received healing energy from the angels.

During the session the client may feel energy moving around or through their body. They may also sense heat, chills, colors, light, geometric forms, dreams, and other visualizations, sounds, memories, and smells. Some people do not sense anything, although this does not mean that the healing has been unsuccessful, as each person responds differently.

Kim is positively affected by every healing. Whenever she works with the angels, she too is healed. Afterward, she feels lighter, happier, and healthier.

Case Study
Karmic Healing

JENN SAID:

I was going through a difficult time, the cliché of trying to "find myself," struggling with my relationship, and raising my son. I was seeking insight as to what path I should take. I was and continue to be in a transition period in my life. I met Kim through another friend and thought she was a wonderful soul, very intuitive, and seemed to have a powerful connection with the angels (which was later confirmed.) I felt an instant connection with her, and felt she was the one to give me this treatment.

The angel past life healing was very empowering. I meditated during the treatment. I sensed a lot. The stand-out memory is that she mentioned that I was in Atlantis and that a little being had taken residence inside my body for protection when Atlantis fell. She could see him and he needed to go home to his own world. Archangel Michael came to get him, and brought him home to his family. I could hear the fluttering of the wings in my ears (the little being was a miniature dragon-like creature,) and a great weight felt like it was lifted.

Also during this session, the first life that we saw was a mountain man who was taking care of me. I was a little boy and he was my guardian. I was carefree, spiritual, earthly, and he was more pragmatic, life and death, black and white. This was a conflict. That man was my partner in this lifetime, and we experienced the same struggles again, and in fact I have this kind of struggle with my father also. It's a lesson that I needed to move through so as not to repeat it, and Kim has helped me greatly with this.

I've dealt with weight and hormonal issues since I was 22 (about 20 years now.) Finding out in this treatment that I lived many lives in poverty helped me to realize that my body carried this from other lives and that the cell memory was of me starving, so they store everything. I have since started slowly shedding some weight. I feel so much more connected spiritually with the angels now, and I call upon them for clarity and protection whenever I can.

Case Study

Karmic Healing

CAMILLE SAID:

While at university I suffered a breakdown. I became severely anxious and felt like I'd lost all connection with my life and myself. I also had a severe rash all over my body that no one could treat. Someone I met told me it could be a past-life issue, so I looked into that. I was searching for an angel-based healing, after having a profound experience at Glastonbury Festival with an angel healer. I looked online for angel healings, and intuitively chose Kim even though she was on the other side of the ocean!

Looking at my life now, I can see that it changed incredibly after the treatment. The information Kim shared was profound and new to me, and touched me on a very deep level. As a result of the experiences I had during past-life healing, I've made many new friends and have enjoyed new experiences.

I have to admit that at first I was very skeptical about the treatment, because I never really believed in angels or psychics prior to my experience at Glastonbury. Yet halfway through the healing with Kim I was sobbing my heart out. It opened me up to much more in life.

The effects of my treatment are still going on today. Because of this reading I'm now involved with new projects and still meeting new people.

I feel truly grateful to have experienced a healing with Kim. She is gifted and warm and funny. She is one of the few "spiritual" people I actually trust, even though we've never met. She opened me up to a new world and I can't thank her enough.

Karmic and Inner Child Healing

In 1995, an angel taught Rekha Vidyarthi interactive healing, with a technique that consisted of prayer and healing process and the client's participation. She has applied the healing process—known as emotional healing with angels—both to heal clients and also to herself, for the past 18 years. This is because the angel told her, "You need to heal yourself in order to heal others."

In 2009, many past lives were revealed to Rekha—not only her own past lives, but also those of her clients—and she was taught how to clear deep levels of negative emotions and past-life karma by changing it, and integrating cleared soul fragments into the higher self, thus shortening the incarnation of a troubled past and present.

Rekha believes that you create your experiences in life, and these experiences provide an opportunity to learn about yourself and heal spiritual wounds. Your outer situation triggers your innermost emotions and feelings. The mind seeks answers, which are often found in childhood, parental imprinting, or a past life. Your angel triggers your remembrance to identify the connection, which is when healing begins. Family karma, anger, fear, guilt, belief systems, and issues of past lives carry over from one life to the next until you heal the issue. A change in perspective makes you take responsibility for creating your experience, and enables you to ask for forgiveness and change the past.

Accessing the inner child

Rekha opens each class or session with clearing prayer. The clients tell her what they want to heal. Usually she can sense if the answer is in the past life, or from parental inheritance through their DNA, or childhood trauma. She asks their angels to bring in their inner child. The client talks to their inner child, making a connection and getting their own answers from their multidimensional divine self. Multidimensional energy spans all planes, timelines, and spaces. The angel triggers the client's memories and feelings, and for some show a past life that is connected to the issue they need to resolve. The client then becomes aware of their lesson, and the answer to their emotional issue or challenge.

ANGELIC HEALING OF YOUR PAST

Resolving issues

Through clearing prayer, Rekha asks to resolve the issue from all past lives and in all dimensions, removing it from the core of the client's being, and generating new, positive beliefs as required.

The client describes what's taking place as angels begin to clear the karmic past. The client experiences both 3D and multidimensional existence simultaneously.

Rekha asks her clients to understand that healing is not always instantaneous. For healing to be successful, a deep level of self-awareness and acceptance is necessary, and it takes time to deal with issues such as anger, fear, and guilt. Once the client understands that they must be an active participant in their own healing, then whatever they experience becomes their own awareness and truth.

When Rekha asked for angelic guidance on her role in the healing process, an angel told her: "You are part of the team of assistance. People like you assist others on physical, emotional, and mental levels. This makes it much easier for us to go in and work on the energetic (quantum) level. What goes on within, affects you at all possible levels. Disease is not outside in, but inside out. When everything within is clean, the body is given the opportunity to emerge balanced, healthy, and energized."

Case Study
Inner Child Healing

I'd been searching for an answer as to why I'd been experiencing anxiety and panic attacks for the last 10 years of my life. I knew that all the energy clearing that I'd done on myself and with friends had helped, but as always, there was more to know and uncover. I was told intuitively to attend a psychic fair in my area, and this is where I met Rekha. While I was waiting for my scheduled reading, I sat next to her and she began to tell me about the work she does to heal people's emotional issues. I was intrigued, and signed up for a session. At the time, I felt harshly judged by my mom and brothers, as their religious belief systems conflicted with my own path to enlightenment. They thought I was "hearing evil spirits." Soon, with Rekha's help I began to see issues very clearly, and how these events had aligned with the karma I entered this lifetime with. I'd felt isolated from my family members in previous lifetimes over and over again. As the scenario was a reflection of me from past lives, I found it easy to forgive once I finally understood. I began to work steadily and consistently with Rekha to get to the bottom of all the heartache of anxiety that I'd experienced. I'd go to sleep and then either toss and turn half the night with palpitations, or awaken an hour or so after I went to sleep with intense fear, and a feeling as if I was surely going to die at that moment. Rekha was my lifeline. I'd call her and she would pray for me with a clearing prayer that we had previously channeled. As I began to ask forgiveness for all the wrongdoings of separate family members from past life events, I could feel that my load was lightening. I'm intuitive and empathic, so I could sense that something was changing within my family unit. Finally, after about a year of these sessions with Rekha, my mother came to my house (she hadn't set foot in my house for over a year because she thought that I might own "demonic" items, ie New Age books), and asked my forgiveness. She confessed that two different pastors/prophets had told her on two separate occasions that she had misjudged me and that I was walking close to God. She brought me a check for $500 as a peace offering, to bless me on my path, and to apologize and ask forgiveness. From that day on, we have shared a beautiful relationship and my mother is now actually opening up and "hearing" for herself. I'll never forget this experience as long as I live.

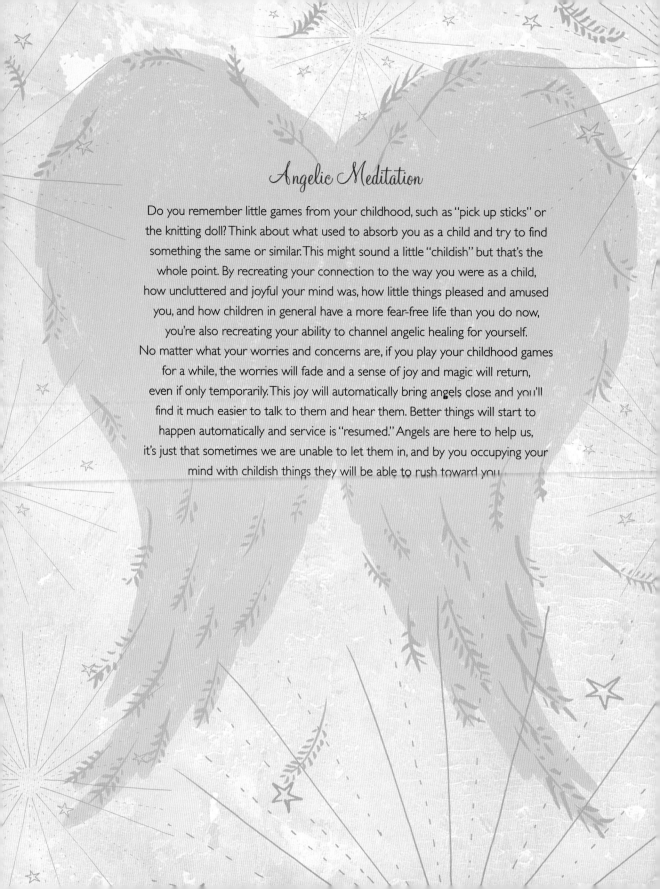

Angelic Meditation

Do you remember little games from your childhood, such as "pick up sticks" or the knitting doll? Think about what used to absorb you as a child and try to find something the same or similar. This might sound a little "childish" but that's the whole point. By recreating your connection to the way you were as a child, how uncluttered and joyful your mind was, how little things pleased and amused you, and how children in general have a more fear-free life than you do now, you're also recreating your ability to channel angelic healing for yourself.

No matter what your worries and concerns are, if you play your childhood games for a while, the worries will fade and a sense of joy and magic will return, even if only temporarily. This joy will automatically bring angels close and you'll find it much easier to talk to them and hear them. Better things will start to happen automatically and service is "resumed." Angels are here to help us, it's just that sometimes we are unable to let them in, and by you occupying your mind with childish things they will be able to rush toward you.

CHAPTER 6

Angelic Core Healing

I DISCOVERED SEVERAL NEW MODALITIES WHILE RESEARCHING THIS BOOK, INCLUDING ANGELIC CORE HEALING. IT WAS WONDERFUL TO HAVE THE OPPORTUNITY TO LEARN ABOUT THIS AMAZING FORM OF THERAPY, AND I WAS DELIGHTED WHEN BRIAN MCCULLEN, WHO DISCOVERED AND DEVELOPED IT, AGREED TO AN INTERVIEW.

Understanding Angelic Core Healing

Brian has been a practicing healer since 1998. He explained that he reactivated physically at the age of 16. This meant that he became increasingly aware of spirits around him. He became involved in prayer groups and religious retreats as he attempted to answer his many questions about the spiritual world. It was at a prayer group that he realized he could channel healing energy through his hands while praying over people. He began to research this experience, and as a result discovered and trained in Reiki. This revealed to him that what he had been doing all along was energetic healing. With this understanding, and an eagerness to learn more, Brian trained in other energy and spiritual healing systems, including integrated energy therapy, crystal healing, angel energy therapy, Seichem, and other more mainstream modalities such as counseling, thought-field therapy, and neurolinguistic programming.

Developing a new system

It was over the course of many subsequent healing sessions with numerous clients that Brian began to receive new healing techniques and methods from the spirit healers and healing angels. He was repeatedly urged by spirits to develop a new angelic healing system, but held back for some time out of fear of bringing a new healing modality into the public arena. Eventually he accepted it, and started to channel angelic messages in the form of healing methods and techniques. Thus Angelic Core Healing® was born, and continues to evolve to this day. While Brian still undertakes limited client sessions, the primary focus of his healing practice now is teaching Angelic Core Healing®, Reiki healing, and crystal healing courses to those interested in becoming spiritual healing practitioners.

Angelic Core Healing® has many angelic patrons, but the main ones are Archangel Metatron, Archangel Ariel, Archangel Michael, Melchizedek, and Merlin.

Angelic Core Healing® works on the client in this lifetime, but it also heals them on a multidimensional level. Multidimensional healing is simultaneous healing across all timelines and spaces—past, present, and future. Angelic Core Healing® heals "all" multidimensional aspects of the client in relation to the issues presented.

Ascension-based healing

This therapy is also an ascension-based healing system, where healing takes place on a physical, emotional, mental, and spiritual level. It also helps to realign the client with their own spiritual source, and brings forth the client's soul consciousness to whatever level and extent is appropriate for them at that time. The therapy differs from other angelic healing systems, because of the extensive training of the angelic healing practitioner and the evolution of their consciousness. Healing meditations and techniques are offered to the clients as a means of helping them to help themselves move into their next space of personal and spiritual growth. A client who receives Angelic Core Healing® is aligned to their own spiritual source, through their own angelic connection, and is encouraged to draw upon their spiritual source. Angelic Core Healing® can be used to treat both physical and emotional injuries.

The Angelic Core Healing® practitioners have been rigorously trained and are very experienced healers. They are able to discern which angelic healing vibrations, frequencies, techniques, and methods are most suited to the client during each healing. In channeling the angelic frequencies, the practitioner calls on the angels, archangel, ascended masters, or spirit guide relevant to the client's issues to step forward and assist with the healing.

Brian commented that when healers channel Angelic Core Healing®, they sometimes glow, and the room may also glow. The healers become more sensitive to light, and see more light around them in the form of energy. This sense of light is caused by working within the angelic dimensions during the session.

Channeling healing energy

The treatment works by the practitioner channeling healing energies from the angelic realm through their energy field, through various angelic light healing rays. The angel healer calls forth and works alongside the angels, as well as channeling the angelic healing rays through the healer's own chakra system and angelic light body. Angelic Core Healing® is both a hands-on and hands-off healing system. The healer will place healing hands on the client's body if needed, and will also give healing to the client's aura and spiritual pathways. The client lies down on a healing table and the practitioner will work around the aura of the client, giving instruction to the angelic healers to assist with whatever comes up during a healing.

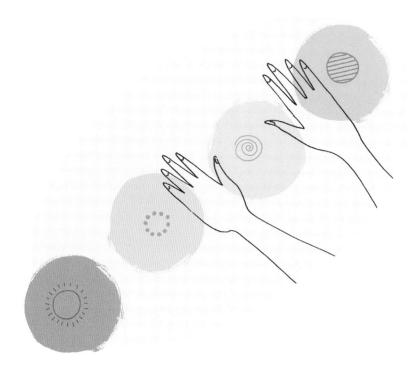

Many clients find the healing energy works very deeply and quickly. They may see colors and experience tingling, and warm and cool sensations, and they may feel as though there are many hands on them at once, channeling healing energy, which is always comforting and soothing for the client.

As a healer, Brian feels tremendous energy during a session. He is aware of the client's angels and archangels standing around the healing space. Various angels and archangels will step forward to assist and give instruction, and partake themselves in channeling the healing energy. As the healer, Brian scans the energy system of the client for blockages in the chakras and energy pathways, and rebalances these areas with assistance from the angels. The angels bring a profound sense of peace and love during a session, and the client will feel this too.

ANNE SAID:

I initially came to Brian several years ago as I had developed some health issues, and I wanted to explore energetic healing as a way of helping myself. Having previously had Reiki healing, I thought I knew what to expect during my first healing, but I was very surprised and delighted by my experience. Brian explained that Angelic Core Healing® uses energy channeled from angels, archangels, and ascended masters. He works multidimensionally, and so heals in a very different way from other modalities. During my healing I found the energy very calming and peaceful, allowing me to relax fully and helping me release any energetic blockages with little or no resistance. ACH is a very powerful energy, and seems to work very quickly not only to reveal the areas that needed to be worked on, but also to start the process of healing and balancing these areas.

After only a couple of healing sessions I was able to feel the difference in the energies, as different archangels or ascended masters came forward to work through Brian and assist in my healings. Brian also gave me meditations and healing techniques that I could use on myself, to continue the healing process between sessions. By giving myself permission to surrender to the beautiful and comforting energy that came through, issues that I had pushed aside and ignored were brought to the surface, healed, and gently released. The fact that ACH also works across many dimensions means that issues are healed across many life-streams at the same time, and so the problem of issues recurring is minimized, leading to the breaking of cycles of behavior, and a freedom to move forward emotionally. ACH has helped me to make many changes to all areas of my life. It has brought me to a deeper awareness of myself, and of my connection to the angelic realm and to the ascended masters, and has truly been a joy and enriched my life. I have absolutely no doubt that anyone open to being healed and willing to move forward can also have their own unique, wonderful, life-changing experiences through Angelic Core Healing®.

Case Study
Angelic Core Healing

UNA SAID:

I went to Brian for an Angelic Core Healing® literally on my knees. I was experiencing excruciating pain in both knees when I walked up the stairs carrying my baby. I lay on a plinth and Brian called in the angels and his healing guides. I felt a sense of deep calm, and could feel a bit of heat and a tingling sensation. The session lasted about an hour, and afterwards I was able to walk with neither discomfort nor pain. I had no more problems carrying my baby upstairs.

Recently I had another Angelic Core Healing® session. This time it was relating to emotional issues from my past. Again I was lying on the plinth feeling relaxed. Brian was working around my head. I could feel pressure and a bit of discomfort around my heart. I received a message from the angels that they were healing my heart. I felt very relieved, and could feel that a weight had been lifted from my chest. I'm happy to say I felt great afterward.

Dear Soul

I know that you humans are struck down with physical and mental illnesses,
which I as an energy being cannot really understand or experience, but I feel
your pain. Sometimes I can't remove your pain from you, although I would love to,
but I can ease your suffering if you take my hand. Just reach out whenever you
need to and you'll feel the warmth of my hand in yours. The same thing will
happen if you're plunged into the throes of grief, another human affliction.
I cannot experience grief for to me no soul ever dies, and I see them forever.
Know that you will be reunited with your loved ones one day.
You can trust me on this.

Your Angel

Angels can be a reflection of your soul. They might not feel the
emotions you feel, but they can't help but know about it. They feel a
shadow of what you feel and will help you when they can.

CHAPTER 7

Angelic Healing Through Cards

ON THE FACE OF IT, THESE READINGS ARE MUCH LIKE ANY READINGS THAT USE TAROT OR ORACLE CARDS, BUT HAVING PAINTED AND CREATED TWO SETS OF ANGEL CARDS MYSELF, I KNOW THAT MUCH DEPENDS ON THE READER'S ABILITY TO CONNECT WITH ANGELS WHILE THEY OR THEIR CLIENT ARE SELECTING THE CARDS. THIS IS PROBABLY THE LEAST INTRUSIVE OF ALL ANGEL HEALINGS I'VE COVERED, AND YET IT CAN BE VERY EFFECTIVE. I'VE SEEN PEOPLE CRY JUST BECAUSE THE WORDS ON A CARD FITTED THEIR CIRCUMSTANCES SO BEAUTIFULLY, AND PERFECTLY ANSWERED THEIR DOUBTS AND EMOTIONAL WORRIES. BELOW, I DESCRIBE THE WORK OF TWO AMAZING CARD READERS.

Silverla St Michael

Silverla St Michael started off by using Doreen Virtue's angel oracle cards. Silverla has always had a connection with and a belief in angels. When she was very young she heard what she believes was angel song at sunrise one morning. She found out more about angels when she did a crystal healing course in 2003–4, and purchased her first deck of cards. They fascinated her, and she started doing readings for friends and family in 2006. She received wonderful feedback from the outset, and her practice quickly grew.

She believes that what she actually does is channeling, rather than just interpreting the cards. Silverla begins by grounding and protecting herself and her client, and then goes into a meditative state to "tune in" to the person she's reading for, by thinking about their name and their questions. She asks the angels for their guidance on those questions. She says she usually "knows" when they are present because she feels a sense of warmth, calm, and peace in her heart, and as an easily stressed person, she finds this feeling very marked. Sometimes she also feels energetic hands on her shoulders and thinks of Archangel Michael. She starts by drawing between two and six cards intuitively, occasionally more, and meditating on their images. She then types out the names of the cards and the brief messages on the front, and then information begins to stream in, usually in the form of snippets, words, and images, which are all simple at first. Then she latches on to one of these pieces of information, and more will come as she types or writes. She has to type or write to do it—it doesn't work otherwise, which suggests there is an element of automatic writing going on, or channeling, as she calls it. Most of the guidance she receives regards how situations can be resolved or improved. However, she also gets glimpses into the future, which she gives people with the caveat that they are just that, glimpses, and our thoughts, actions, and decisions can make positive changes all the time. Silverla has now carried out hundreds of readings and, in her own words: "I'm humbled by the gift I have, and so grateful for it, as I know I've touched people's lives and brought them comfort at a time when it was most needed. So many people have given me feedback to say they recognize exactly what I'm saying about their life at the time of the reading, and some even come back later and let me know that what I predicted had come to pass."

Case Study
Angelic Healing Through Cards

MELANIE SAID:

I met Silverla on an Internet message board unrelated to spiritualism, and she quickly introduced me to her gift. At first I did it just for fun, but soon afterward I found myself dealing with some serious challenges in my personal life, and turned to Silverla to help me sort it all out. Her readings have always been very accurate, positive, uplifting, and full of hope. Her words made me think of the bigger picture, and past the pain I was feeling in the moment. She was always there to answer any questions and further explain when I felt confused, and to support and encourage me. I feel that the readings she did for me were a major part of what got me through a horrible time in my life. Then, she introduced me to the "angel letter." She asked me to write a letter to the angels asking for their help. She then blessed it, and channeled a response. I had thought only her readings were powerful, but to read the words spoken from an angel was an experience like no other. The readings felt like a gentle hug, but the letter was like having Raphael grab me by the shoulders and look me in the eye, peering into my soul, making sure I heard the message that was being spoken directly to me. It was an amazing experience. Silverla is an incredible woman with a heart of gold, who I believe came into my life for a reason. She has touched my soul and opened my eyes to something I never knew I needed.

Case Study
Angelic Healing Through Cards

CAZ SAID:

I'd been feeling a bit lost in terms of life direction, and felt a reading would perhaps give me some motivation or guidance that something "good" might be on its way. I chose Silverla because when I looked at her information and picture I got a good honest feel about her. I then sat quietly and "asked" if she would be able to help me. At the time I had this feeling of "go for it, she will give the guidance you need." Silverla emails the readings to you within three days. She told me things I'd not expected her to know, which surprised me. I'd been kind of closed-minded to readings, but was happily surprised with what she told me. It made me realize that there was a higher power/angels involved, and that she definitely has a gift. From one of her readings in December 2009 she told me that I would conceive a baby girl in 2010. I thought my family was complete, but had a surprise pregnancy and went on to have a beautiful healthy baby girl. She also told me not to worry about the money issues I'd been having, as there would be money coming to me mid-2010, and again it did happen! In May 2010, a surprise early inheritance came through and solved our financial worries. I was incredibly surprised and happy with her reading, and that's why I continue to work with her to this day.

Serena Empath

Serena Empath remembers happily conversing with spirit guides as a child of seven years old, although she didn't believe in angels with wings in the conventional way. Her belief in them came out of the blue while she was at university in 1997. She was walking home one night after 2am, and had to walk through a very dark and lonely wood. Unfortunately for her, there was a suspicious-looking man watching her, and she kicked herself for staying out so late. Then, to her surprise and delight she sensed two very tall muscular men walking next to her, as if they were her bodyguards. An immediate feeling of calm washed over her, which she now knows was thanks to the presence of angels. The men didn't speak, but their presence dissuaded the stalker, and he turned his attention away after following her a little bit more. She called the men "my angels who watched over me," and vowed never to walk home alone late at night again.

I paint angel portraits for people on my Facebook page, but I don't have time to "read" them for the people they're done for. Serena Empath is one of those who have very kindly taken up the reins and she does the readings for me. She uses the portraits in much the same way as people would use angel cards. I asked her to describe in her own words how she reads the images: "I just look at your beautiful paintings, and the images come to life. It's not just the one angel that I see there, but patterns within patterns that seem to dance to life. As claircognisance (the gift of psychically knowing information without being told in a conventional way) is my strongest gift, I am able to intuit information and simply write it down. In addition, I feel things when I connect to your reader's energies and I write them all down. If I'm struggling to understand, I use oracle cards to assist my understanding, and always tell clients when I have used them."

Case Study
Angelic Healing
Through Oracle Cards

ZRINKA SAID:

Serena made me think about myself a lot, about things that I need to change and
the things that I should put first. I received good advice about listening to my intuition and was also
told not to be so controlling. I really feel that the reading was honest, and Serena didn't hide the truth.
She tells it as it is, with no pretense.

Case Study
Angelic Healing
Through Oracle Cards

CAROLINE SAID:

Serena gave me a wonderful reading of the angel that Jenny drew. It was very accurate, especially as she picked up on my animal healing work and the fact that the angel was connected to the ocean (a week before Serena's reading, I had another psychic reading and learned that my personal guide was a water goddess). Serena was also able to give me the name of my beautiful angel, which is "Ulvas," which means she has another connection to the sea. I was able to form a really close connection to my angel after Serena's reading, as I felt I understood her much better. Serena is a very gifted angel reader, and her reading has given me much strength and a deep personal connection to my angel.

Case Study
Angelic Healing Through Oracle Cards

LISA SAID:

I could relate to everything being said. Serena saw a dolphin in my angel, and I have a dolphin tattoo on my back. I can also relate to the words Serena wrote regarding taking things for granted, and that gives me great guidance to make sure that doesn't happen in the future. Communication is key for me, as it has been my biggest challenge, but these words give me reassurance that if I trust my gut instinct, I won't go wrong.

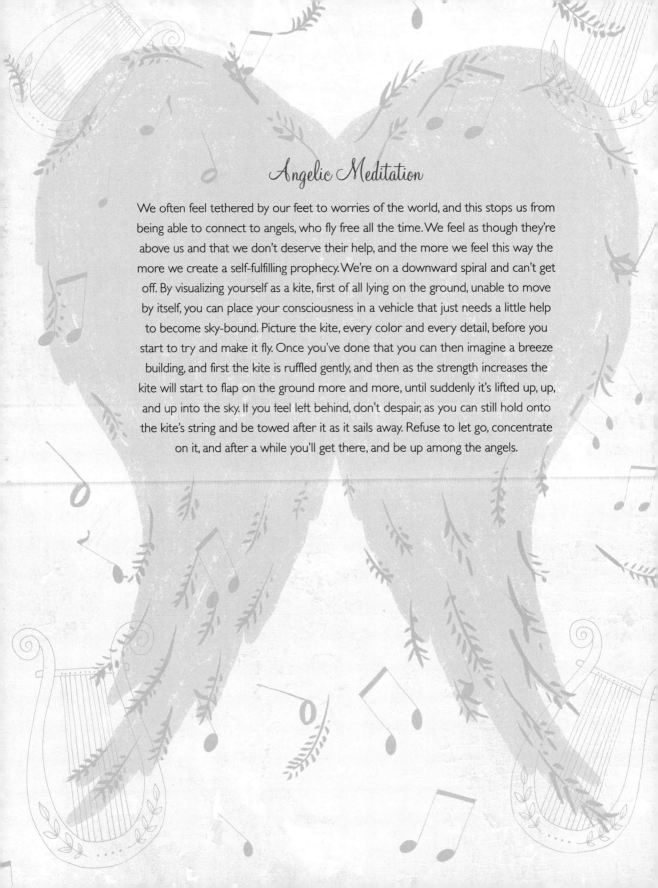

Angelic Meditation

We often feel tethered by our feet to worries of the world, and this stops us from being able to connect to angels, who fly free all the time. We feel as though they're above us and that we don't deserve their help, and the more we feel this way the more we create a self-fulfilling prophecy. We're on a downward spiral and can't get off. By visualizing yourself as a kite, first of all lying on the ground, unable to move by itself, you can place your consciousness in a vehicle that just needs a little help to become sky-bound. Picture the kite, every color and every detail, before you start to try and make it fly. Once you've done that you can then imagine a breeze building, and first the kite is ruffled gently, and then as the strength increases the kite will start to flap on the ground more and more, until suddenly it's lifted up, up, and up into the sky. If you feel left behind, don't despair, as you can still hold onto the kite's string and be towed after it as it sails away. Refuse to let go, concentrate on it, and after a while you'll get there, and be up among the angels.

CHAPTER 8

Angelic Energy Healing

I'D NEVER HAD ANY PERSONAL EXPERIENCE OF THIS MODALITY, SO I WAS INTERESTED TO DISCOVER EXACTLY HOW IT WORKED. FULL-SPECTRUM VIBRATIONAL ENERGY TREATMENTS HEAL HOLISTICALLY, WHICH MEANS THAT THE WHOLE BEING (PHYSICAL, MENTAL, EMOTIONAL, AND SPIRITUAL) IS TREATED, RATHER THAN JUST A SPECIFIC PART OR SYMPTOM. THIS TREATMENT USES ENERGY, CRYSTALS, AND SOUND TO SURROUND THE WHOLE PERSON WITH AN AMBIENCE IN WHICH THEIR NATURAL SELF-HEALING ABILITIES CAN OPERATE AT THEIR FULLEST POTENTIAL. INTUITION IS ALSO ENHANCED DURING THIS TREATMENT, CREATING THE PERFECT ENVIRONMENT FOR HEALING, RESTORATION, AND RELAXATION. IT IS A PROCESS OF "LETTING GO" OF THOUGHTS AND FEELINGS THAT ARE NO LONGER HELPFUL TO US.

The Healer's Experience

Steve Clayton always enjoyed helping people whenever the opportunity arose, but didn't realize what a positive effect he could have on the wellbeing of others until he discovered full-spectrum vibrational energy healing. His wife, Kim, helped him to recognize his innate ability, and encouraged him to study energy healing. He went on to study several energy modalities, including Reiki, crystal healing, and sound healing. This process helped to expand his (naturally) limited five-sensory view of the world. It also introduced him to the angels. What his left brain might have once scoffed at, he was able to embrace whole-heartedly with the help of angels. He felt the angelic energy in his heart, and also discovered an ability to differentiate between the archangels themselves, from Michael's forceful presence to Raphael's gentle energy. When he began to call on the angels for assistance during healing sessions, they responded by telling him the treatments felt more powerful and that a loving partnership was formed. He knew then that he had found his life's purpose. The more he worked with the angels, the more his awareness expanded, and he realized he was not limited to helping people in the here and now, but could also help them in all directions of time and in multiple dimensions. From the beginning, people have told him that he is "out there." He replies by placing his hand over his heart and saying, "No, I am in here and it feels terrific."

No two healings are the same

Steve explained to me that no two healings are ever the same, but there are basic practices that he follows for all clients. To begin a healing session he grounds himself to Mother Earth and, if applicable, to the patient's planet of origin. (It's a less known belief that some people feel they can remember lives on planets other than this one. Indeed, some people believe we all originated elsewhere. This information is provided intuitively by Steve's angelic guides.) He then asks to become a crystal-clear connection and channel for the energy. He invites Archangel Michael to clear away negative energy from his client and himself. He also asks Archangel Raphael to help guide the session, and remains open to receiving help from any angels or spirit guides who may wish to assist. Since all healing comes from love, he requests that his higher self help keep him in his heart, and asks the person's higher self for permission to facilitate the healing. After this, he sets the intention to heal on all dimensional levels and in all directions of time, releasing everything that isn't for the person's highest good. Then he simply allows the angelic energy to flow through him, guiding him as it deems fit.

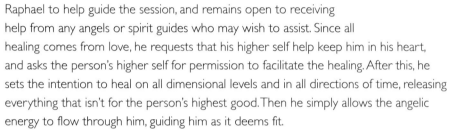

Letting go of expectations

When I asked Steve what he expects a client to get out of the session, the honesty of his answer surprised me. He said that he doesn't have expectations when it comes to healing. He says he discovered very quickly that everyone experiences these sessions differently and the same person can have a totally different experience from one healing session to the next. So, instead of implanting expectations, he asks clients just to clear their minds as best they can, or to think and feel only loving thoughts.

Steve says that he too is affected positively by every healing he undertakes. He experiences a sense of calm and peace that washes through him. This is the tricky part he takes pains to express: "When I teach about healing, I stress that if a healer is using his or her own energy during a session, they will feel drained during and/or after the session. They may also feel as though they are going to spontaneously combust. Conversely, if a healer feels 'charged up' after a session, then he or she may be (unknowingly) taking a lot of the energy for themselves, rather than allowing it to flow into their client. A healer is a facilitator and a witness, rather than being the actual source or cause of the healing. During a healing session, the angels calm me, guide me, and occasionally give me messages to relay to the patient. I ask for, and gratefully receive, whatever help they wish to give me."

Case Study
Angelic Energy Healing

JENNIFER SAID:

My main reason for seeking treatments is for migraines and depression. I met Steve Clayton and his lovely wife, Kim, at a holistic wellness fair. Kim introduced me to Steve, and I was immediately taken by his natural charisma. Steve is friendly and warm, with a great sense of humor. I immediately felt at ease and safe with him. I was comfortable sharing my thoughts and feelings with him, which is very important when it comes to having a treatment. I once told Steve I needed a treatment because a certain person's existence was driving me over the edge. Steve listened to me seriously, had a little good-natured chuckle, and then got to work.

My experience was warm, welcoming, and healing. Knowing that I'm an animal lover, Steve allowed his dog Tux to remain in the room for the treatment, which I really appreciated.

I always feel so much lighter and calmer after a session. The anger and sadness are dissipated. The energy causing the migraines has been cleared so that I can function once again. I feel grounded.

Steve's hands are very warm while he works. I've felt energy shifting during a treatment. Sometimes this is a pain in my ankle, a twinge in my knee, or an ache in my back. I'll mention these sensations to Steve and he does what he can to correct the pain. During one treatment there were some very energetic forces acting. Steve had placed a crystal near my crown chakra (top of the head,) slightly underneath the pillow. When he went to work on my head I heard the crystal hit the floor. Steve chortled. I thought Steve had knocked the crystal on the floor. Apparently, the energy shot the crystal across the room!

At the end of the treatment Steve is always happy to explain what he said or did. It's nice to know that your chakras are back in balance, or that your guardians were present.

I definitely believe others can benefit from treatments of this kind. If people are open to this experience there is no reason why they can't benefit from a healing with Steve. I find as time goes on I need treatments less often as the effects are long-lasting, and underlying problems are resolved. These treatments also help me to develop coping mechanisms and to be more aware of myself and my surroundings.

I am very happy to have met Steve. He is a very powerful and humble healer.

Case Study

Angelic Energy Healing

GINETTE SAID:

I was suffering from the very painful condition of fibromyalgia. I'd followed all kinds of treatments previously, medical, homeopathic, and two years of Reiki. I chose Steve as the practitioner to try next because of his wonderful, calming, soft energy. The treatment made me realize that there was more help available than I'd thought. It gave me more confidence that I could be treated, and that full-spectrum vibrational energy could work, and it really did help. I continued to feel the calming and healing effects of his treatment for weeks after. I can still easily recall the feeling of the energy on my body and chakras. Emotionally, it calmed my nerves. My spirit was also greatly improved and the healing opened up another path spiritually for me.

Distant Angelic Energy Healing

For this treatment, as its name implies, you don't have to travel to be with the therapist. This might seem a bit odd, but it really does seem to work and does suit some people.

Linayah Kei

During a healing session, Linayah acts as a bridge for energy to come through to her client. When she is given the go-ahead to do so by the angels, she goes to the computer and channels all the information and messages into an email that she then sends to the client. These are lengthy emails and take her over an hour to write. There's so much information that it takes time to absorb it, and each time the client reads it they get more from it.

Linayah's sessions are very personal, and bring the love and healing energy from the angels to her client. She starts with an initial, free consultation to discuss the treatment in detail and answer any questions that the client may have. During the session, Linayah works remotely and suggests that her clients might like to sit or lie down in their own space, ensuring that they are comfortable and have privacy. Linayah usually finds that a client's guardian angel will introduce themselves during the first session, and pass on messages to her that she can then relay to the client via email.

These sessions are not known as "readings" as Linayah does not "read" anything, but instead simply provides a space that the angels can enter. After a session, Linayah is always available for any follow-up questions from the client, and maintains a continuous flow of contact so that the client's needs are fully met.

I wanted to get one of my therapists' "take" on how they personally work with angels, and how angels make them feel, as this would give people a better idea of what's in store if they too can make a connection through a healing modality. I chose to ask Linayah Kei how she felt:

"My love for angels is very deep. They're always with me and speak to me in many ways. I view them as my friends, beloved friends, and can't imagine not having them in my life. I always know the angels have my back no matter what happens in my life. My work with the Archangels is still evolving, and Archangel Michael is my best friend, and the one I call my main guide. I even have loving names for him, "Big Mike", and my "Wingman." He speaks to me continuously and sometimes has to be a bit loud in order for me to listen! He's loving and powerful and yet still very funny. I'm a channel, in other words angels 'download' information to me to pass on to others. I use automatic writing, and this means I'm channeling a book with the angels about angels, and the illustrator is also channeling the artwork. I love having the words of the angels flow through my fingers so that I can share them. I'm also a voice channel. This again is a very fulfilling way to allow angels and spirit to speak through me. Being a vessel for them to come through and relate their messages is lovely. I'm very grateful and humbled that they've asked me to do this."

Finally, I asked Linayah to share some of the knowledge she's been given about angels with my readers:

"Angels love us unconditionally and never, ever tell us what to do or not do, but instead hold us in love and protection, and give us loving guidance on opportunities and possibilities that are there for us. They also never tell us what we have done wrong, for they see no mistakes. We have Free Will and Free Choice so we can follow the guidance or not. And if we do not, that's okay and there's no judgment or less love. No matter what we do or say, angels will always love us unconditionally. I tell everyone that once they allow the angels into their lives nothing will be the same again. We all have many angels that are with us and when I can help them introduce themselves to someone, it gives me a feeling of great joy and I always smile, for I remember when that happened to me."

Case Study
Distant Angelic Energy Healing

LINDA SAID:

At the time of my first session with Linayah, I was feeling overwhelmed and depressed. I was struggling with faith, or lack of it, and I was in need of hope and encouragement. I'd been on my spiritual journey for a few years, and more recently had taken risks and made efforts to improve my life. I followed my heart, changed careers, and earned a Master's degree. However, I still felt dissatisfied, as my outer life circumstances appeared largely the same. I remember feeling as though my soul was "broken" after divorce, and raising two sons on my own, one with special needs.

My session with Linayah brought great emotional peace into my life. It helped me to understand, and then change my thought process. I was able to embrace the "bigger picture" about my life and the truth about who I am. I felt uplifted, loved, and supported, with a more positive outlook on my life, and could more confidently make changes in my beliefs about myself. I accept that I am a spiritual being having a human experience, not a human with a soul. I now understand that my thoughts create my experiences, and that programming from society had shaped those thoughts. This awareness makes a big difference in the way I perceive the world around me.

Case Study
Distant Angelic Energy Healing

KATHI SAID:

Three years ago, I was in search of some deep spiritual healing because I'd suffered the great loss of my husband, and was totally exhausted and depleted with grief. I couldn't seem to heal myself, and needed some help. The first reading I had brought me love, relief, and joy. Of course I still mourned, but I felt a greater understanding of how the universe and angels worked alongside us if we asked for help. My more current readings are more about guidance for a future that I couldn't see myself having before. I started to get excited at the prospect of the rest of my life, instead of dreading it. The love, guidance, and encouragement from the first few healings helped to set a foundation for future growth and spiritual expansion, and later healings have guided me to more advanced spiritual work and healing by opening new ideas and doors.

The divine is just waiting to be asked. The angels love to help, but they also know we have free will, so will not intervene without being asked. My most recent reading opened many, many new doors and my growth has been exponential. I'm truly grateful for all the blessings, filled with love and joy from learning about new angels, new masters, new continents, etc. I am open always for the next step, and feel greatly healed since my first healings three years ago.

Dear Soul

Special love for a human partner is a strange thing for me to understand because I feel the same amount of love, which is boundless, for every other being in existence, whether they are human or animal souls. So, when you mourn the loss of a lover, or you crave a partner who understands, it's sometimes hard for me to not just look at the bigger picture. So if you need help in this regard, be persistent, and your dreams can come true. But you must trust that if someone walks out of your life, it is because they are meant to. I often have to watch while you block your rightful partner, whom I have found, from coming into your life, because you are clinging to a love that is spent.

Your Angel

An angel's love is all you really need to be whole, and an angel's love is there for you at all times. Love other people, of course, but depend on your angel and stand strong even when you are alone.

CHAPTER 9

Angelic Multidimensional Healing

ANGELA ARNOLD AND FRAN MORRIS ARE EXPERTS IN THE FIELD OF ANGELIC MULTIDIMENSIONAL HEALING, AND I WAS DELIGHTED WHEN THEY AGREED TO SHARE THEIR EXPERIENCES.

Angela Arnold

Angela initially learned Reiki, and taught that, followed by past-life regression and spirit release. This led her to angelic Reiki, which she also went on to teach. But as wonderful as all of this was, something was always still "missing" for her; the picture was incomplete. When her angelic Reiki master announced that she had put together a system known as angelic multidimensional healing (AMD,) Angela knew that this was going to be the piece to make her "soul sing." For Angela, angelic multidimensional healing challenges all the limits and confines we place on ourselves, living in our three-dimensional world, and lifts us beyond that if we are willing to trust and to let ourselves live as we are meant to—in love, harmony, and truth. Angela says: "I now consider myself to be a child of the Multiverse, and as that child I allow myself to move beyond limitations, to learn and to experience all, and thus bring back the experiences and energies for all who encounter me. My expansion and learning continue every day, as my heart grows fuller and fuller with love."

Working with the higher consciousness

Angela's work begins as soon as a client makes the decision to come to see her. By making the energetic commitment to have a session of AMD healing, the higher conscious mind is working with the client's guiding angel to ensure the outcome is for the highest good at that time. When the client arrives, they talk to Angela about why they have come, and what they would like to achieve for themselves. When the session starts, Angela merges with the energy of her own assigned healing angel, and together they merge with the energy field of the client. She does not invite any other energies into the session, other than the guides of the client. She leaves all the decisions to the healing angel, who, after all, knows far better than anyone. Angela is simply a facilitator who, by expanding her own energy body, is capable of holding universal, angelic, and galactic energies. The more she develops herself, the higher the energies she is able to hold in her energy fields, and the greater the benefit for the client. The energy is

channeled via Angela to the client, and is received by them on whatever level it's required, whether that be the emotional, physical, spiritual, or mental body, or a combination of these elements. The energy may feel hot or cold, and is often experienced as a kaleidoscope of colors, which Angela sees as the "energetic signature" of the being working with the client at the time. The client nearly always sees the same images as Angela. When the beings have finished the healing that they have come to do, they close it down and seal it in, and the healing will continue to work at various levels for between three and four weeks at a time, such is the depth. It is both profound and life-changing.

The healing effect

I asked Angela to reflect on how the healings affect her personally: "Every session is different. It is always blissful. I love to work with the energetic beings; a lot of them are with me time and time again, but always interspersed with ones who are new to me. Sometimes I am very in the earth with the connection, and sometimes I am out in the cosmos; other times I could be with one of the many stars from the constellation. It all depends on the client. Sometimes I am swept along with the love and peacefulness of it all, just as the client is sometimes held in suspension, so too am I, although I am in total trust with my healing angel, my gate-keeper, and my protectors so we are all totally protected at all times. We are always surrounded with light. I look forward to every session with my clients, as it is lovely to connect in this way with the many beings who are always ready to work with us, and to whom my healing angel is always willing to make an introduction. Angelic multidimensional healing is my heart."

JESSICA SAID:

I'd been going through a real dark patch in my life, and nothing seemed to make sense anymore. I'd suffered low self-esteem and self-love issues from childhood, and had looked for escapism through recreational drugs and partying; although it had offered short-term gratification it certainly didn't fix the problem for long. After starting a new job in which Angie was my colleague, I decided to book myself in for an AMD healing session. I had no previous knowledge or insight into what it was to be spiritual, and certainly wouldn't have called myself religious. When Angie placed her hands on me for the first time I had this incredible surge of energy rush through my body, which felt like electricity. I couldn't believe what I was seeing, because even though I had my eyes closed I could see magenta, gold, white, and the most amazing purples I'd ever seen. I wondered if the lights had changed color or something. The most immediate sensation was the feeling of peace and love that rushed through me that was so intense that I began to sob uncontrollably, and I realized that this was what it was like to have an "awakening." It absolutely changed my life. I went from being a typical party girl with a carefree attitude to most things, to realizing that the answers are all buried deep within us, and we just don't allow ourselves the space and love to heal ourselves. I changed my lifestyle completely, and spent time alone doing some soul searching and understanding the esoteric self, chakras, angels, spirit guides, and tapped into a whole new world I never knew existed. It was like being reborn. I know now that we're all divine beings in a state of remembering our divine nature, but we get so bogged down with trying to fit into society and being accepted by the people around us. AMD helped to channel pure loving angelic energies into the very center of my being, making me feel connected and balanced again. I believe that we're all made up of energy and are accumulated from this life, as well as past lives. It is up to us to unravel that and connect with our soul path. Making a connection to our true selves is the very purpose of self-development and ascension.

The experience has made me more self-aware, and also you naturally become more clairvoyant and aware of other people's feelings, as this is part of the ascension process. It may not be the same for everyone, as we all have our own unique energies and gifts.

Case Study

Angelic
Multidimensional Healing

LOUISE SAID:

What triggered me to go to Angela was that I'd left my old life in London, together with a job I'd had for 13 years. I'd gone through a painful relationship breakup and this was the year for changing my life to how I'd dreamt it to be. I was going to spend six months in India, learn to be a yoga teacher, and then move to Brighton, all on my own.

Every AMD healing experience is different for me. The first one I had felt like my heart was breaking, almost as if pain was being pulled out of it, and I knew it was a release. On that occasion, my heart was being healed so it could be open for my journey ahead. Angela did not know at the time that I was planning a six-month trip to India. The next session was much softer and I saw lovely colors. This time was all about clearing anything that needed to be cleared for my journey, and then protection from the violet flame, which Angela told me I could call upon if ever I felt I needed it. I have called upon the violet flame ever since when I've felt a bit scared. After both sessions I really felt ready for my adventure and starting my new life.

Fran Morris

When I talked to Fran Morris, it was brought home to me that every therapist puts their own slant on the various treatments, which goes to show that angels are diverse and wonderfully inventive in the guidance they bring, making it suitable for many different kinds of people.

Fran had already used Usui Reiki and found it beneficial as a form of healing. She was also becoming more aware of the presence of angels in her life, so when she found out about AMD healing it seemed to her like a natural progression. She started first of all by using the system on herself, and found it incredibly powerful and beneficial to her on all levels—physically, mentally, emotionally, and spiritually—and particularly helpful with finding and following her life plan (that which we came here to accomplish and follow.) She told me that her friends noticed how it was transforming her and her life, and then asked if they could have a treatment from her. When they too experienced wonderful results, this led her to practice as a therapist and then teacher of the system, in order that she could pass this incredible gift on to as many people as possible.

How the treatment works

I asked Fran what exactly a treatment involved, and this was her definition: "The therapist is attuned to the frequency of the angelic realm, and at this time experiences an angel stepping forward to become their healing angel, and will be working in partnership with them from that time onward. When giving a treatment the therapist asks their healing angel to merge with them, and from then on, throughout the treatment, the therapist simply acts as a bridge between the angelic realm and the client. Any number of angels can then be called in, together with ascended masters and galactic healers of the light, depending on what is appropriate for the client's highest healing at that time. As the therapist I am able to "watch" what healing they are bringing in for the client to some extent, and can then relay any information I receive back to the client after the treatment, which is often helpful. The treatment is multidimensional and can work on past lives, as well as the past, present, and future of this life, and work on any issues, whether physical, mental, emotional, or spiritual. It really is all-encompassing to an extent that we may almost struggle to comprehend."

The client's experience

The session begins when the client is asked what they need help with, and they are then made comfortable on a therapy couch (fully clothed), although the treatment can be given to someone sitting in a chair if necessary. Soft music is generally played. The hands-on part of the treatment can last anything from 10 to 30 minutes. Some clients just find it very relaxing and seem to "drift off." Many see colors, and some see images. Clients sometimes say they can feel other beings present during the treatment. It's also common to experience physical sensations such as heat and areas being worked on in the physical body. Some say they feel as though they have just had a whole night's sleep. The treatment can continue to work for several days afterward so the client is encouraged to take particular care of themselves after the session. They are offered a glass of water immediately after the treatment, as this can help continue to cleanse them and ground their energies. Some clients have reported to Fran that their circumstances also appeared to change, for example by them becoming aware of new opportunities coming forward, or by them perhaps realizing that certain areas of their life might benefit from changes being brought in, and then realizing that they now have the strength to do this.

Case Study
Angelic Multidimensional Healing

MIKE SAID:

I've suffered with fibromyalgia in varying degrees for 50 years, and this has become worse with age. The cause of this condition was unknown. I felt drawn to AMD healing while I was in a desperately painful state. Other forms of conventional medicines/drugs and alternative therapies had systematically failed to arrest the condition, or give any prolonged relief of the symptoms. I was very impressed from the first treatment (and I'm not easily impressed.) Emotionally I felt calm and safe, and physically I experienced sensations of localized heat where treatment was being applied. I had tingling, palpitations, and a deep feeling of relaxation. I remember on my very first treatment that a severe pain in my head, similar to migraine, which had plagued me for years, seemed to just melt away.

After several more treatments addressing the underlying causes, the pain of my fibromyalgia hasn't returned. I'm now free of the debilitating pain I had suffered for 50 years. Before, I was unable to have a life, as most people would understand it, because of the constant pain. I was restricted in what I could do. Exercise was limited to very short walks. Stress only brought about more pain, which restricted me still further. Eventually I was forced to retire early, as working in an office and socializing with people became almost impossible because of the pain. But now I'm able to conduct my life as others do. For the first time in many years I can walk longer distances, work in the garden, drive long distances, and have meaningful relationships. It is not unreasonable to say that my life has been transformed by AMD.

I'm humbled by the healing that's taken place. I'm now much more emotionally secure and self-assured, as well as being less stressed and fearful than before. When I think back even 12 months to the depths of despair and pain, and the very dark place that I'd inhabited for many years, I'm now a totally different, much more relaxed, and positive person than before.

Case Study
Angelic Multidimensional Healing

KAY SAID:

I'd been feeling stuck and lost in terms of my career, and also unable to fully let go of the fact that I had wasted some time in this rut, but without any sense of where I wanted it to go, for a long time. It was a kind of vicious circle, but what really concerned me was that this had begun to eat away at my confidence. I needed a completely new direction, but could not see a way forward. My old friend, who'd experienced amazing transformational results (physically and emotionally) from the treatments she had received, and from subsequently having become a therapist, offered me a treatment when she was visiting me for the weekend, and I thought I'd give it a go.

The sensation in this case was quite remarkable. I'm not sure if it was because I needed a strong sense of the treatment "working" that the feeling was so marked, but I felt absolutely submerged in a very warm, strong touch, as if being "held" by wings, throughout the treatment. My mind raced in very visual dreamscapes (unlike me—I'm quite a word-driven and logical person,) and afterward I felt very calm, reassured, and in some way lighter than I had felt in a very long time. It was exciting. I felt that something had definitely shifted in me.

I'd asked for healing for my highest good, and stated that I was open to any change, but I asked if my working life and my ability to earn steady money could be protected no matter what changes needed to take place in me. (My confidence was low. I'm not sure what I was expecting to happen!)

The irony of this has never failed to amuse me, when I consider the events that ensued from the treatment. Afterward, I felt able to say consciously to myself that I was open to any opportunity that came to me, and no matter how bizarre or challenging it seemed, I promised to myself I would say "yes" to it. I knew that this would give me the opportunity to find the right direction, and the confidence I had almost completely lost in myself.

And bizarrely, opportunities started coming my way immediately. I found myself
with a huge amount of freelance work to do, using new skills that I'd been developing
in the background from work, without ever realizing where they'd lead me. I was then
contacted by an old college friend and asked if I'd act in a training film he was making for the
company he worked for, and I immediately said "yes."

During the filming of this I met the managing directors of the company, and everything clicked into place.
They ran a really inspiring business, with an ethical model and a unique management and training philosophy.
The place just felt amazing to be in when you entered their office (I'd started doing some freelance work for
them). I loved the work they did and I knew I wanted to work there.

To continue my story, I was writing an open letter to the managing directors of this company just six weeks after
meeting them, to say I'd like to work for the company (and was open to a change of direction)—when one of
them called me and said there was a senior management role open and asked if I would come and see them for
an interview! I got the job, which was wonderful. Three years on, I'm now a director of the company and have
never been more fulfilled in my career.

I've since taken the course in AMD so that I can self-treat and treat others (friends, family) when
the opportunity arises. I am delighted to have the skills now so I can use this work whenever I like. I find
the daily discipline required for good practice is very beneficial and energizing
(and takes no more than ten minutes a day).

In subsequent treatments, I've been able to receive greater clarity on all kinds of issues, which has
enabled me to progress and to liberate myself from habitual patterns of thinking and
feeling. This has helped in my personal and professional life.

Angelic Meditation

One of the most powerful and positive emotions we can have when it comes to connecting with angels is being in awe of beauty. Find yourself a spot that inspires you and use it for contemplation. The Earth is a beautiful place, and we can all find somewhere we appreciate. Spectacular is good, like a wonderful, white-sanded beach (Holkham Bay in Norfolk is one I love) or a stunning vista such as you'd see from the top of the Quantock Hills in Somerset, but it can equally be a really pleasing group of trees, a rushing river, some flowers, or a view of a distant peak. The important thing is to sit or stand and let the joy of your love for the Earth take you over. This kind of emotion will create a cocoon of perfect positive energy around you and draw angels to you like a beacon. Once you feel their beautiful energy, let your awe of it surround you and ask for what you need. Then all you have to do is believe that it will be granted, and it will be. The form of the gift may differ slightly from what you think you want, into what you actually need, but it will make you happy.

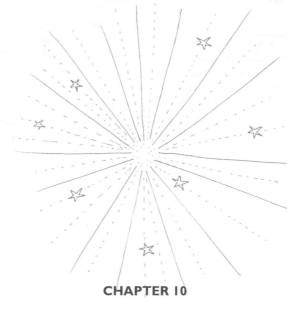

CHAPTER 10

Angelic Healing
for Pets

MADELEINE WALKER PRACTICES WHAT SHE CALLS ANGELIC
EMPOWERMENT HEALING FOR PETS. SHE IS A TRUE PIONEER IN THIS
FIELD AND WORKS WITH ANIMALS AND HUMANS, HELPING THEM TO
RESOLVE PAST-LIFE TRAUMAS. SHE WORKS INTERNATIONALLY, RUNNING
CLINICS, PERFORMING READINGS, AND FACILITATING COURSES IN
ANIMAL COMMUNICATION AND HEALING. SHE TRAVELS EXTENSIVELY
TO WORK WITH WILD SPECIES IN THEIR NATURAL HABITAT, AND IS
PASSIONATE ABOUT CONVEYING THE MESSAGES SHE INTUITS FROM
THESE WISE CREATURES, GAINING WISDOM FOR PLANETARY HEALING.

I spoke to one of Madeleine's clients, Victoria, about her experience.
"I went to the wonderful Madeleine Walker for a healing session for myself and
both my dogs. I left the dogs in the car so that we could concentrate on me
first—most unusual for me as I usually put myself last. One of the first things
Madeleine said when we had sat down was that she had taken her dogs for a
walk just before I arrived, and had seen two white feathers joined to look like
wings glistening in the frosty sunshine. Marveling at their beauty, she went on a
few paces and saw another set of joined white feathers. She was guided to pick
them up and bring them to put on her healing altar. Madeleine was also guided
to use her crystal bowl to do some sound-healing and remove any negative
blocks from me. Madeleine sat on the floor with the bowl, and she said that from
the beginning she felt hands on her shoulders directing her and keeping her to
know what to do—she was told it was Archangel Michael. I could feel an
amazing presence in the room—it was truly awesome. Archangel Michael
showed Madeleine a past life of mine where I was a powerful warrior goddess,
and said that I had come into this life as a very gentle, humble being but that I
had given too much of my power away and I needed to reclaim it. With the help
of Archangel Michael directing Madeleine with the crystal bowl, we had an
amazing sound-healing session with me being guided to release the frustration
and anger that had been buried so deeply. It was truly wonderful and I felt free. I
was then able to assist Madeleine in healing my dogs when it was their turn. The
dogs requested healing from me rather than Madeleine, as they wanted to prove
to me that I could do it, and Archangel Michael was guiding me through this as
well—it was a way I had not used before. He was a very strong presence for me
that day and for quite a while afterwards to remind me of my power."

Be Orford

Be is another animal healer, who calls on two specific angels before beginning any animal communications. An angel portrait artist told her about these angels several years ago. One is Angel Beatrice, who wears a coat woven with flowers and is strongly connected to animals and nature. The other angel has not yet revealed his name, however Be has seen him briefly during a meditation. These are Be's two companion angels.

For Be, a visualization prior to the communication can be particularly interesting as she is only fully in control at the start of the visualization, and does not know who will appear to help and guide her. Her guardian angel usually takes the form of a winged horse and is always present, helping to keep any negativity away. The angels show Be the type of healing that is required (emotional or physical.)

Be recounted a beautiful healing experience that she had with a neighbor's cat. "The cat always tried to live in our house, as they weren't all that fond of him in his own home. This cat had a few physical and emotional issues to deal with, and sometimes he acted up, wrecking the house and bothering our other two cats. I had always had a fairly complex relationship with this cat. I welcomed him in during the winter and was happy to feed him, but there were also times when I had to ask him to leave. I felt quite bad about this inconsistency, as the poor cat didn't know quite where he stood with me. He started to pretend to be part of the furniture so that I wouldn't notice him and ask him to leave. One day he came into the house and sat beside me on the sofa. I started to apologize to him for the inconsistency in my behavior. I felt strongly connected to the cat and, the next moment, an angel appeared in front of us, blessing us both. It was a powerful healing experience for both of us, and something I think of often."

Jackie Weaver

Jackie is a well-known animal healer, who has worked with many celebrities' pets. I asked Jackie to share some of her experiences as a healer: "How many times have you said your animal is an 'Angel on Earth'? I have heard it many times, not just from the human owners, but also from the animals themselves. I hear messages from living animals, and also from animals in spirit.

Every animal comes into your life for a reason, and they often teach you important lessons. Sometimes they come into your life when they are really needed, and open your heart and mind in unbelievable ways. Many are quick to tell me that their owner has psychic ability to communicate telepathically, and they want them to help other animals too—such a precious and natural gift to be shared. As they live their life as an animal angel, whether on this planet or in heaven, they desire you to be happy and go forward in your life, and they will do all they can to make it happen. Often when a young animal goes to heaven and once you have to cope with their passing, you find that they will be there to guide you in work that they know you can do. We owe it to them to do our best; after all, they tried their best for us.

Working with Spirit

Sometimes animals can be fearful in various situations, and I will call upon my mare in spirit to help. She was lively and bold, and she taught me a lot. When I first started to communicate with animals I quickly rushed to apologize to her for getting "this and that" wrong. I smile as I recall how quick she was to tell me, "We make mistakes too!" Sometimes while talking to another horse that is consumed with fear, I ask my mare to come forward and share her strength and love with that horse, in the hope that they can take comfort from her. Just because you can't see an angel doesn't mean they are not there. Whether they are of human form, or appear as animals that have graced this earth with their wonderful presence, the thought that we are being watched and often guided brings peace in itself.

I will never forget the first time an animal told me of an angel. The emotion I can remember, and feel, to this day. I had started out doing a communication with a horse and talking about various aspects of his life with his lovely owner. He was cheeky and funny, found life easy, and had no real worries.

During the conversation, we touched upon a traumatic moment in their lives. One day, many years ago, the owner was enjoying a day out with a friend, both riding their beloved horses. Something spooked the horse and he bolted and ran straight into a cattle grid. The poor horse was now stuck, unable to get up and

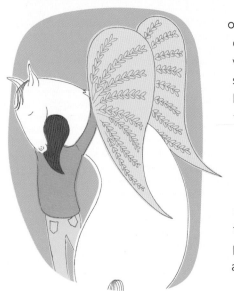

out of this metal trap, miles from anywhere, with his owner crying by his side. Fortunately, the other rider who was with them was able to call the fire brigade and vet. By this stage, the panicking horse was really struggling to free himself and, with tears flowing, his owner positioned herself to lie under his head. This was for two reasons—firstly so she could hold and comfort him. Secondly to stop him damaging his head on the metal bars as he desperately fought for freedom. The fire brigade arrived, but they could not do anything to help free the horse without causing severe damage to his legs. By now, the horse was so tired from struggling, it looked as if nothing could be done but put him out of his distress. A vet was also now in attendance, and ready to carry out the deed.

During our communication, the horse's owner asked me if her horse had any memories or anything to share from that day. I gently asked the horse if he would be willing to communicate about such a traumatic event. Almost instantly I had a vision of him lying down trapped by the grid, and then, suddenly, rising up and standing tall alongside everyone else. This vision was accompanied by the words, "The angels lifted me out." I asked the owner if this resembled what had happened and, stunned, she told me it was exactly as things had occurred: one moment her beloved horse was collapsed, exhausted, and trapped, and the next he was standing up, totally unharmed. The firemen and the vet were amazed, and could give no explanation for what had happened.

When an animal angel comes into your life, cherish whatever time you spend together on this earthly plane every day. However they came to you, believe me, spirits will guide them to you. You were destined to be together. So when your angel does indeed return to heaven, remember these words as said by one of them, "We never leave you, we just become an unseen part of you."

True Stories of Angel-Sent Animals

Angels can offer help and healing comfort in many ways, in many guises. Animals can be sent to offer solace, comfort, and company, and the very fact that they need us to care for them can lift us out of the doldrums and trigger our self-healing abilities. Animals can also be used as messengers from our passed-over loved ones, and help us to heal from grief.

Case Study
Angelic Healing for Pets

ANGELA SAID:

When I lost my dear dad, I hoped that he'd still
find a way to give me good advice as he always used to
do when I had a problem. I love horses, always have done, and
years ago I had a fantastic pony called Misty. I had no fear of him and we
had wonderful times together. He made me think that having my own horse was just pure
joy. However, when he died I started to realize that a partnership like that would be very hard
to find again. I had several horses on loan and was injured several times in riding accidents, until I
totally lost my nerve and thought I should "hang up my hat" for good.
I still used to look at adverts offering horses for loan, but I didn't really think I could ever get my nerve
back to ride again. Then one day I saw an advert offering a "happy hacker" called Zack, for loan. There
was no photo and I didn't know whether to risk going to see him, so I sat and stared at my dad's photo,
asking him for help. I honestly felt an answer surge through me to "go for it," so I did.
When I first saw Zack, he didn't look great as he had been wintered out and had suffered for it. He had a
lovely, kind nature, though, and I felt at ease straight away. I watched the owner and her young daughter
ride him, then I rode him myself and I felt that my father was watching over me. I felt safe, and very happy.
I knew he was for me, and I would enjoy spoiling him as he deserved.
I've not had that feeling with any other loan horse I have tried. I only have him two to three days a
week and he's still stabled with his original owners. He is old now at 22, but we're maturing
together. His owner is lovely and says he's more like mine now. Last winter I kept him in at night,
and he looks really well now, although during the winter he did have some health issues and
I was truly devastated to think that he might not make it through. But he did, and
everyone comments on how good he looks. I think that we keep each other
happy and well. I wish I could have a conversation face to face with my dad
about him, because he would be very happy for me, as he knows
how much it means to me. I truly believe that he knows,
and that his advice was angel-sent.

Case Study
Angelic Healing for Pets

ERICA SAID:

I got my angel-cat Benny in December 2003 as a
nine-week-old kitten. He was the runt of the litter, but
I chose him because he was unable to do what the other two were
doing, as he wasn't strong enough. He was so tiny and so beautiful, I fell in
love with him immediately, and it became obvious to me very quickly that this relationship was a
very special one and involved some kind of soul connection.

I'd had two and a half years' worth of very bad relationships—one with an emotionally abusive cocaine
addict, and another with a duplicitous alcoholic and sex addict. Both relationships contributed to a period
of depression and overwhelming sadness.

Benny turned out to be my savior. This ball of fur and fluff made me laugh out loud with his naughtiness and
cheekiness. He comforted me beyond any love I could ever comprehend or imagine. In moments of utter
despair when I had just had enough, Ben would wander in and snuggle up beside me and sleep with me till I felt
human again. He brought me gifts aplenty—mice, birds, spiders, frogs, and bats! He was a great joy and made my
life much more bearable and happier. He could be so naughty, but could win me over in a nanosecond with a tilt
of his beautiful head and a stroke on my face with his paw. One funny thing was that he refused to have a collar
on him, and if I managed to get one round his neck, he would delight in flicking it off with his paw and dangling
it in front of me. I came to realize eventually that he was trying to tell me that he didn't need a collar to tell
him that he belonged to me.

A few hours after we moved into a new house, he got out and went off wandering,. I was frantic with
worry, but after an hour or so he came sauntering round the corner without a care in the world.
How did he know the house? He hadn't ever seen the front of it. Then I realized that he
knew me and would always know where I was, as he was part of me.

I met my now-husband, Adam, not long after I'd sworn off men for
good! I'd known Adam since I was 10 years old as he was one of my
brother's best friends, but it took him 38 years to ask me out! Ad was a dog man
and came with a rescued lurcher called Victoria, who was gorgeous if more than a little
scatty. She was afraid of most things except cats—and after Ben got over his initial outrage at
having a dog in the house, they became, if not friends, tolerant of one another. Sadly we lost Victoria
just before we all moved in together, and we were all very upset, including Ben.
Ben won Ad over by lying across him in the mornings as if to say, "This one isn't going anywhere!",
and Ad won Ben over by feeding him! Ad became a proper cat lover because of Ben.
Ad and I married after five years together, and we were blissfully happy. Just six months after our wedding, only a
week before Christmas, Ben died from antifreeze poisoning. He lay on my chest on the Friday night and I knew
there was something wrong, but not enough to be able to know if I could do anything. But as he lay on me, just
staring at me with his big eyes, I suddenly just knew that this was "it." It was such a strong feeling that I knew he
was going to die—but it turned out there was nothing anyone could do about it. I now realize that he was saying
goodbye. At the vet's, as he was dying, I stroked him and instinctively told him that he could leave now and soar
with the angels. I cannot begin to tell you the devastation Ad and I felt. I could hardly comprehend the loss of
my soul companion, because that was what he was. I didn't understand at first the total and utter feeling of
loss and bewilderment when suddenly he was gone. My little cat—my baby—gone. I became ill with
shock at first, and then struggled to accept what had happened. As much as I tried it seemed
incomprehensible that he had gone. After a period of deep, deep
mourning and grief, I can't help but think that Benny came—or
was sent—at a time when I was really struggling and
needed help, and when I was settled and happy,
he left—just like that.

The week he died, I believe I had two visitations from him. Two nights after
he passed, I had the most vivid dream in which Benny told me not to feel bad or
guilty—but it was his time to go and he had been called back. There was absolutely nothing
I could have done. Five nights after, I had another extremely vivid dream in which he walked up a
path to me, looked up at me, and said, "Hello Mom, I'm back."

The house that had been so spiritually dead that week definitely felt warmer and less soulless, as if
something had come back to life. Even Ad commented on the atmosphere, and he is generally quite closed
to that kind of thing—although he does believe that Benny was a guide for me and that now he has left me in
Ad's capable hands. I do understand that—but for a long time I couldn't understand why Ben couldn't have
stayed. I realize now that I have things to do. I've picked up again my long redundant reflexology and Reiki
business and although I'm not inundated yet, I've finished my therapy room and I'm ready to go, with interest
starting to come in. I'm also looking into some form of animal healing. I do believe that Benny had to get me to a
stage in my life where I was happy, and therefore able to open my mind to continuing what I started years ago. I
just wish I could have done it with him here, but I guess the laws of spirituality don't work like that. I can feel his
warmth and love in my therapy room, and weirdly, our rescue cat, Little Bear, won't go in there! It really has
taken me a good six months to get over my absolute grief. I felt as if I had lost part of myself—my heart was
broken and I didn't feel that it would ever mend. I cannot write with enough feeling what this furry boy
did to my soul—he completed it and with his loss, it felt broken. I've read avidly, and at one point
obsessively, about animals and the afterlife—where has he gone and why did he have to go? I
believe absolutely, without a doubt that he was my soul companion—sorry—is my soul
companion. I just don't know if he was sent by the angels or if he was the angel!
Whichever way it is, I can still feel him, and pray one day for his return.

Case Study
Angelic Healing for Pets

AMANDA SAID:

I was a single mother with two children, and I had
depression and felt very alone. Even though I had wonderful
friends and family around me, I don't open up to people very easily. Then
my cat Simba had to be put to sleep, and when I took him to the vet one of the nurses
there had a kitten she'd rescued. The kitten had been born feral but was now domesticated
and needed a home, so I took her to try and help my daughter with the grief of losing Simba. We
called her Pixie. Everyone who met her said she was special, that she wasn't "just" a cat, and that she
radiated love and warmth. We had an immense connection that I've never felt with any other animal,
and she followed me everywhere, missing me when I was gone. She was like one of the children, sitting
with them when they had picnics, sitting near us at the dinner table, and she even came to find me when
one of them cried. When I had my baby last May she would continuously sit near her, guarding her,
especially when the midwife came. She was very protective over the baby and had to be close when
anyone came to visit or held her. Pixie was there to love and comfort me, without needing anything from
me. She was with me until I met my now-fiancé (my twin flame) who helped me through my depression,
and gave me unconditional love and support as well as a new baby.
Sadly Pixie was run over and killed when my baby was only two weeks old. I think she knew it was
time to leave me because I'm so busy with the baby, who in turn has helped me through the grief. I
feel a massive void in my life, but I feel blessed that she was with me for the three years I had
her. At first I was angry that she'd left, but now I realize what an amazing gift she was. She
came to me when I really needed her; now that my life is happy and complete it is
time for her to go and be there for someone else. Selfishly I want her back
because she was a huge part of my life, but I truly feel honored that she
chose to be with me, and I know that we'll be reunited one day.

Angelic Meditation

What is imagination? Why do people say "it's just your imagination?"
To me the imagination is a facet of your higher self. Many creatives such as artists,
authors, and song-writers will tell you they have no idea where their ideas come
from—past lives, messages from angels, predictions? We don't know but
I do know that the imagination is a great tool for meditation, especially where
angels are concerned. So, use yours to make a connection with angels.
Your visualization knows no bounds; you can see in your mind's eye a strange
world where you're happier and stronger and "be" there for a while, or you
can people your mind with tiny beings like the Borrowers, whatever will capture
your attention. These may be "just stories" but they will give you the right kind of
energy to bring you to the attention of angels. Whatever story you imagine
for yourself, make it as detailed and personal as you can, because the more you
make it your own the better it will work for you. Suddenly, you realize that
you're not alone in the make-believe and the presence you sense will be your
angel, so then is the time to communicate.

CHAPTER 11

Can You Change Your Life with Help from the Angels?

I HOPE THAT THE HEALING MODALITIES DESCRIBED IN THE PRECEDING CHAPTERS HAVE GIVEN YOU AN INSIGHT INTO THE AMAZING WORLD OF ANGELIC HEALING. THERE ARE SO MANY FORMS OF HEALING TO CHOOSE FROM THAT YOU ARE SURE TO FIND ONE THAT WORKS FOR YOU.

My Story

I truly believe that you can make dramatic changes in your life almost instantly with the help of the angels. About 18 years ago you would not have recognized me. I didn't believe in anything really, especially not myself. Despite having what most would consider to have been a "good life," I was very depressed and feeling adrift, unable to get up in the mornings. If you've ever felt this way, like me, you might eat to "cheer yourself up," and of course, like me, become overweight, which will only make you feel worse. I felt worthless and couldn't be bothered to do anything about it. Life was a waste of time. And yet I still felt there was something I was meant to do, something that would give my life meaning if only someone would tell me what it was.

But then I came to believe in angels. I had an angel speak to me. I had angels appear to me, and a miracle came to pass, in fact many miracles came to pass. I lost weight without dieting. I felt energized and powerful. I started writing song lyrics and won an award for it, and I had a past-life experience that led me into writing books. I became a local TV presenter, I earned enough money for my beloved husband to leave work in time to get treatment for and recover from an illness, I started writing for magazines, and my story of awakening was in the national press worldwide. I was offered this path by angels and I accepted it.

Our Angel Energy

A lot of people say that you don't get help from angels unless you're in the right energy state, and many times this is taken to mean a "happy" state. Most of the time this is correct. However, I'm living proof that sometimes the right energy state can be flat and featureless, dull and calm. When we first feel low or scared, our reaction is often a sense of desperation and helplessness, or a rush of adrenalin so that we can try to escape what we're afraid of. I believe that it's when we get beyond this to a state of acceptance of our situation, and total naked hopelessness, with all our normal thoughts scattered to the wind, that occasionally we can reach out to angels where they exist. They suddenly hear us in our silence, when before we've been too busy screaming out in pain or terror for them to. I think this explains why people in extreme life-threatening situations get help. Their energy isn't happy at all, but once they've gone past the initial horror they feel about their situation and passed into a numb void of feeling (similar to that which a mouse is said to be in when trapped by a cat), that is when they're heard and a miraculous rescue can take place. That was how it was with me. Just when I'd reached rock bottom, an angel suddenly spoke into my ear and said, of all things, "Turn the TV on." This of course is not the heavenly, dramatic thing one expects an angel to say, and if I had been in my "right" mind at the time, I might have ignored it. But by then I was almost robotic, and just carried out the instruction without thinking about it. I needed to see someone who was on the TV at that moment, in order to recognize him from a past life. The miracle in me was wrought not precisely by this recognition, but by the far deeper recognition that there truly was much more to me than I'd ever dreamed. I truly was immortal. I truly did have a soul. I truly was a divine being.

Of course, it's much more pleasant and easier to create calm energy within yourself and talk to your angels that way.

I'm not suggesting that everyone could follow this particular path of depression, nor that they would actually want to, but most of us are searching for a meaning, for that important thing we're sure we're here to do. Angels can help with this dramatic kind of transformation, if we can only connect somehow, whether our destiny is to become a wonderful gardener, a fantastic mother, or the President of the United States. Angel healers can help with this immensely.

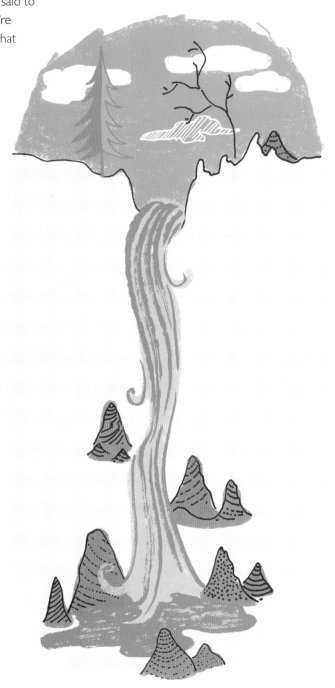

Change Your Life in Gradual Easy Steps

You can change your life in simple everyday ways, to maintain and strengthen your connection to angels.

Develop a "switch" that you can literally click within yourself to get instant angel communication, or that your angel can trigger to let you know they are close.

These "switches" can take many forms, and to develop one that is reliable and helpful is just a matter of practice and self-training. You can decide on your own signal, or your angel can provide you with one. This symbol or sign can be chosen or given during meditation. When you feel you have a deep connection, ask or say what this sign should be. Listen to your intuition, and go with the first thing that comes into your mind.

If you select one yourself, it could be

1   A word you say when you need your angel
2   A place you go to when you need help
3   A certain color you wear when communication is needed
4   A number you repeat in your mind until your angel comes through
5   A certain song or poem you repeat

If your angel selects one for you, it could be:

1   A feeling of cobwebs on your face
2   A gentle brush of wings
3   A feather or flower that appears at your feet
4   A shiny coin
5   An angel-like cloud or a rainbow

When you have your sign, train yourself to "switch off" the world immediately when it comes or when you call it in. Shut out all thoughts and believe. Once you've practiced this enough, you'll be amazed how you can call upon your angel anywhere, at any time. The more you do it, the more it will happen, and the easier and more instinctive it will become.

Change Your Life Slowly

Develop an understanding of how it's necessary sometimes to be patient while asking for help. If you think of all the people in the world who are right now asking for help, you'll come to understand what a complicated place we live in. In order for everyone to have what's in their best interests, many things must fall into place for them, while at the same time no one else can be dislodged from their rightful path. Little things can change a lot for many people, so time, care, and planning have to go into what angels want to help with. Understand that although things will take time, in time they will come to be.

Change Your Life by Being Grateful

The happier you can feel today, the happier you will be tomorrow. The very best energy for getting help more quickly is to feel genuine gratitude for what you are about to receive. If you live as if your dreams had already come to pass, then they will come to pass more quickly. This is partly to do with the fact that we can create our own reality, and partly because it creates the kind of energy that angels not only tolerate working in, but positively feel ecstatic in.

How Do You Know When You've Made Contact?

Angels use all our senses to make contact. Some angels communicate through our sense of hearing. Some people actually hear voices in times of stress, as I did, perhaps giving them words of hope that they're being guided in the right direction to escape from their problem. You might hear some song lyrics, which might seem coincidental and yet resonate with you so much that they can bring an angelic answer. Like me, you might feel urged to turn on the radio or TV at a certain moment, and hear some sung or spoken words that mean something to you.

Some angels communicate through our sense of sight. Countless people have described the same images, without ever having spoken to one another. Visions of angelic beings usually happen when you're in a meditative state, as this condition renders one's energy receptive.

Sometimes angels will use our sense of touch, usually with featherlike gentleness. This sign can be as subtle as a soft breeze when there are no windows or doors open, and no drafts.

Even our sense of smell is used by some angels. For instance, my mom, who passed many years ago, still uses angels to come through to me at times, and her presence is always announced with the smell of freesias.

Then we move on to the less-used senses. Angels can use your psychic senses to allow you to write unconsciously. This is called automatic writing and drawing.

A sense of being loved is probably the most cherished of all signs of angel presence. Your emotions can be used by angels, too. Anyone who has had an angel in their presence will have experienced the all-encompassing, nonjudgmental, and eternal feeling of love and compassion that washes over us when angels enfold us in their energy.

Angels can come to you in dreams. Keep a pen and paper beside the bed to jot down anything that comes to you in sleep as soon as you can, as these messages can be forgotten.

Colors can signify that angels are close. For instance, some people experience a beam of violet light. The colors can vary, though, and often you'll find your answer by looking up the meaning of the color you see.

The ways of communication are many and varied, and this is where an angel healer can step in to get you started.

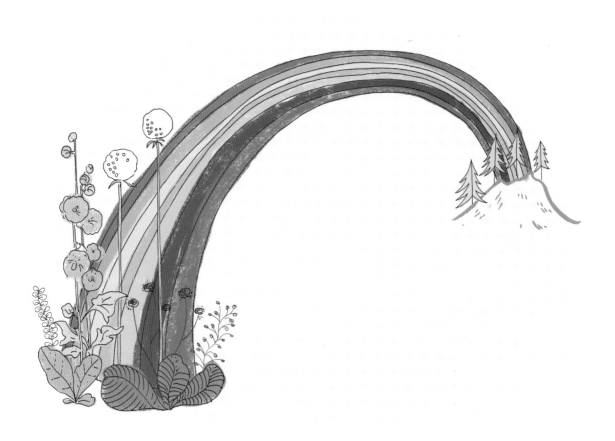

About the author

Jenny Smedley, DPLT (Diploma in Past Life Therapy), is a qualified past-life regressionist, author, TV and radio presenter and guest, international columnist, and spiritual consultant, specializing in the subjects of past lives and angels. She lives with her husband, Tony, a spiritual healer, and her reincarnated "Springador" dog, KC, in beautiful Somerset, in the UK.

Her life was turned around by a vision from one of her past lives, in which she knew the man known today as Garth Brooks, the country music singer. Problems relating to that life were healed and resolved in seconds. By following the guidance she received from her angels, among other things, she became an award-winning songwriter overnight. Her angels enabled her to overcome a lifelong fear of flying to go to the US to meet Garth Brooks, so closing the circle.

For two years she hosted her own spiritual chat show on Taunton TV, and her guests included David Icke, Reg Presley, Uri Geller, and Diana Cooper. Jenny has appeared on many television shows in the UK, US, Ireland, and Australia, including *The Big Breakfast, Kelly, Open House, The Heaven and Earth Show, Kilroy,* and *Jane Goldman Investigates,* as well as hundreds of radio shows, including *The Steve Wright Show* on BBC Radio 2, and *The Richard Bacon Show* on Five Live in the UK. She has also guested on the radio in the US, Australia, New Zealand, Iceland, Tasmania, the Caribbean, South Africa, and Spain.

Here are some comments that the national press have made about her:

"**Unique rapport with the natural world.**" *Daily Express*
"**A global phenomenon.**" *The Sunday Times Style* magazine
"**World renowned for her ability to use angels to help people.**" *Daily Mail*

Jenny's website is www.jennysmedley.com. She'd love to hear from you about your own angel experiences, so please get in touch by emailing her on author@globalnet.co.uk, and perhaps your story will be immortalized in another of her books. Please also join Jenny on her Facebook page for instant conversation with her and her friends: www.facebook.com/JennySmedleyAngelWhisperer.

Jenny Smedley is the author of many inspiring books:

Past Life Angels

Past Life Meditation CD

Souls Don't Lie

The Tree that Talked

How to Be Happy

Forever Faithful

Supernaturally True

Pets Have Souls Too

Angel Whispers

Soul Angels

Everyday Angels

Pets Are Forever

Angels Please Hear Me

A Year with the Angels

My Angel Diary 2012

An Angel By Your Side

Soul Mates

My Angel Diary 2013

My Dog Diary 2013

My Cat Diary 2013

My Angel Diary 2014

Resources

Angela Arnold www.angelaarnold.co.uk
Ceri-Ann Beecroft www.the-food-angel.co.uk
Glenda Bouchere www.togetherwithangels.com
Nikki Byford www.kaleidoscope-holistic-therapies.co.uk
Steve Clayton www.clayhuthealing.ca/index.html
Serena Empath http://serenaxthomas.com
Angela Hahn http://www.angelichealingschool.com
Kim Hutchinson www.clayhuthealing.ca/index.html
Linayah Kei http://www.angelicpathtohealing.net
Brian McCullen http://www.angeliccorehealing.com
Silverla St Michael http://spiritualsolace.webeden.co.uk
Fran Morris http://www.joyunlimited.co.uk
Be Orford Email be.orford@facebook.com
Carol Ann Powell http://www.onangelwing.co.uk
Rekha Vidyarthi www.emotionalhealingwithangels.com
Doreen Virtue www.angeltherapy.com
Madeleine Walker www.anexchangeoflove.com
Jackie Weaver, author of *Celebrity Pet Talking*: www.animalpsychic.co.uk

Index

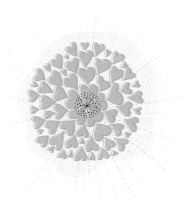

Acknowledgments

I'd like to thank Lauren at CICO for her unstinting work, which has helped me to produce such a beautiful book.

I'd also like to thank Trina Dalziel for her gorgeous interpretations of my words into images.

My thanks also go to the therapists and their clients featured in this book for their generous contributions.

Whatever happens in your life, never doubt that angels exist and that they care for you. Some people have an innate ability to connect with their angels, while some of us need a little more help. I hope I have shown you where this help is available, and I would love to hear from you about your experiences with the healing angels.